Table of Contents

```
// Spring Security configuration for authentication @Override
protected void configure(AuthenticationManagerBuilder auth) throws
Exception {     auth          .inMemoryAuthentication()
.withUser("user")
.password(passwordEncoder().encode("password"))          .roles("
```

Chapter 1: Introduction to Java

1.1 The Java Language

Java is a high-level, object-oriented programming language that is designed to be platform-independent. It was created by James Gosling and released by Sun Microsystems (now owned by Oracle Corporation) in 1995. The language was developed with the goal of providing a platform that allows developers to write code once and run it anywhere, a concept often referred to as "Write Once, Run Anywhere" (WORA). This is achieved through the use of the Java Virtual Machine (JVM), which interprets Java bytecode on different platforms.

History of Java

Java's history dates back to the early 1990s when a team at Sun Microsystems, led by James Gosling, started working on a new programming language project. The initial goal was to create a language for programming consumer electronics, but Java soon found applications in a wide range of areas, including web development, enterprise software, and mobile app development.

The official release of Java in 1995 marked the beginning of its popularity. Java's "applets" brought interactivity to web browsers, and it quickly gained traction as a versatile and secure language for web applications. Over the years, Java evolved, with new versions and features being introduced to meet the changing needs of the software development community.

Setting Up Your Java Development Environment

Before you can start writing Java code, you need to set up your development environment. This typically involves installing the Java Development Kit (JDK) and configuring your code editor or Integrated Development Environment (IDE). The JDK includes the Java compiler (javac) for compiling Java source code into bytecode and the Java Runtime Environment (JRE) for running Java applications.

To install the JDK, you can visit the official Oracle website or use alternative distributions like OpenJDK, which is open-source and freely available. Once the JDK is installed, you'll need to set the JAVA_HOME environment variable to point to the JDK installation directory.

```
export JAVA_HOME=/path/to/your/jdk
```

Your First Java Program

Let's start with a simple "Hello, World!" program in Java to get a feel for the language. Open your favorite code editor and create a new file called HelloWorld.java. In this file, enter the following code:

```
public class HelloWorld {
    public static void main(String[] args) {
```

```
        System.out.println("Hello, World!");
    }
}
```

This code defines a class named `HelloWorld` with a `main` method. The `main` method is the entry point of a Java program. Inside the `main` method, we use the `System.out.println` statement to print "Hello, World!" to the console.

To compile and run this program, open your terminal, navigate to the directory where `HelloWorld.java` is located, and use the following commands:

```
javac HelloWorld.java
java HelloWorld
```

You should see the output "Hello, World!" displayed in your terminal.

Java Development Tools

Java offers a rich ecosystem of development tools to streamline the software development process. Some popular tools and IDEs for Java development include:

- **Eclipse**: An open-source IDE that provides a comprehensive development environment for Java, including code editing, debugging, and project management.

- **IntelliJ IDEA**: A commercial IDE known for its intelligent code assistance and deep integration with various Java technologies.

- **NetBeans**: An open-source IDE that supports Java development along with other programming languages.

- **Maven**: A build automation and project management tool that simplifies the building and managing of Java projects.

- **Gradle**: Another build automation tool that allows you to define your build process using Groovy or Kotlin DSL.

- **JUnit**: A popular testing framework for writing and running unit tests in Java.

These tools, along with the vast Java community and extensive documentation, make Java a powerful and developer-friendly language for a wide range of applications.

In this section, we've covered the basics of Java, its history, setting up a Java development environment, and writing a simple Java program. In the subsequent sections of this book, we'll delve deeper into Java's features, libraries, and advanced topics. Stay tuned!

1.2 History of Java

The history of Java is a fascinating journey that begins with its origins at Sun Microsystems and continues to shape the software development landscape to this day. In this section, we'll explore the key milestones and events in Java's history.

Birth of Java

Java's story begins in the early 1990s when a team of engineers at Sun Microsystems, led by James Gosling, embarked on a project known as the "Green Project." The primary goal was to develop a programming language that could be used for programming consumer electronic devices, such as set-top boxes and interactive televisions. The team recognized the need for a language that was platform-independent and could run on a variety of hardware.

Oak Language

The initial result of the Green Project was a language called "Oak." However, Oak was eventually renamed to "Java" due to trademark conflicts with another company using the name Oak. The name "Java" was inspired by coffee, as the team enjoyed Java coffee from a nearby coffee shop.

Release of Java 1.0

The first official version of Java, Java 1.0, was released to the public in January 1996. This release included many of the core features that define Java to this day, including the Java Virtual Machine (JVM), the Java Standard Library, and the applet technology for web browsers.

"Write Once, Run Anywhere"

One of Java's revolutionary concepts was the idea of "Write Once, Run Anywhere" (WORA). Java achieves platform independence by compiling source code into bytecode, which is executed by the JVM on different platforms. This approach allowed developers to create software that could run on any device with a compatible JVM, regardless of the underlying hardware and operating system.

Java's Rise on the Web

Java quickly gained popularity as a language for developing dynamic and interactive web applications. Applets, small Java programs embedded in web pages, brought interactivity to the web. However, as web technologies evolved, JavaScript became the dominant language for web development, and the use of Java applets declined.

As Java continued to evolve, it expanded into the enterprise space with the introduction of Java Enterprise Edition (Java EE). Java EE provided a robust framework for building scalable and secure enterprise applications. It included technologies like Servlets, JavaServer Pages (JSP), and Enterprise JavaBeans (EJB).

Open Sourcing of Java

In 2006, Sun Microsystems open-sourced Java under the terms of the GNU General Public License (GPL). This move led to the creation of the OpenJDK (Java Development Kit), which is now the reference implementation of Java. Open-sourcing Java contributed to increased community involvement and the development of alternative Java distributions like OpenJDK and AdoptOpenJDK.

Oracle's Acquisition of Sun Microsystems

In 2010, Oracle Corporation acquired Sun Microsystems, becoming the steward of the Java platform. Oracle continued to release new versions of Java and introduced a new release cadence, with regular feature updates and long-term support (LTS) releases.

Recent Java Versions

Recent versions of Java have introduced significant features and enhancements. Java 8 introduced lambda expressions and the Stream API, making it easier to work with functional programming constructs. Java 9 introduced the module system, and Java 11 marked the first LTS release under Oracle's new support model.

Java's history is marked by its adaptability and enduring popularity. It has found applications in a wide range of domains, from web development to mobile app development, enterprise software, and more. As we explore Java further in this book, we'll dive into its features, libraries, and best practices, ensuring that you're well-equipped to harness the power of this versatile programming language.

1.3 Setting Up Your Java Development Environment

Setting up a proper Java development environment is crucial for efficiently writing, compiling, and running Java code. In this section, we'll guide you through the steps to set up your Java development environment, including installing the Java Development Kit (JDK), configuring your code editor or Integrated Development Environment (IDE), and managing dependencies.

Installing the Java Development Kit (JDK)

The first step in setting up your Java development environment is to install the Java Development Kit (JDK). The JDK includes the Java compiler (javac) for compiling Java source code into bytecode and the Java Runtime Environment (JRE) for running Java applications. Here are the steps to install the JDK:

1. **Visit the Oracle JDK website**: You can download the Oracle JDK from the official Oracle website. Alternatively, you can use open-source alternatives like OpenJDK.

2. **Download the JDK**: Choose the appropriate JDK version for your operating system and download the installer package.

3. **Install the JDK**: Run the installer package and follow the installation instructions. During the installation, you may need to specify the installation directory. Make a note of this directory as you'll need it later.

4. **Set the `JAVA_HOME` environment variable**: After the installation is complete, set the `JAVA_HOME` environment variable to point to the JDK installation directory. This variable is used by various Java tools and applications to locate the JDK. Here's how you can set it on Unix-based systems:

   ```
   export JAVA_HOME=/path/to/your/jdk
   ```

   On Windows, you can set it through the system properties dialog.

5. **Update the `PATH` environment variable**: To make the `javac` and `java` commands available globally, you should add the `bin` directory of the JDK to your system's `PATH` environment variable. On Unix-based systems, you can do this by adding the following line to your shell profile (e.g., `.bashrc`, `.zshrc`):

   ```
   export PATH=$PATH:$JAVA_HOME/bin
   ```

   On Windows, you can add the JDK's `bin` directory to the system's PATH via the Control Panel.

6. **Verify the installation**: To verify that the JDK is installed correctly, open a terminal or command prompt and run the following commands:

   ```
   java -version
   javac -version
   ```

   You should see information about the Java version and the Java compiler version.

Choosing a Code Editor or IDE

Once you have the JDK installed, you need a code editor or Integrated Development Environment (IDE) to write and manage your Java code. There are several options to choose from, depending on your preferences and needs. Here are a few popular choices:

- **Eclipse**: Eclipse is a widely used open-source IDE known for its extensive set of plugins and features for Java development. It offers a rich development environment with code highlighting, debugging, and project management.

- **IntelliJ IDEA**: IntelliJ IDEA is a commercial IDE by JetBrains, known for its excellent code analysis and intelligent code assistance. It offers a free Community Edition and a paid Ultimate Edition with additional features.

- **NetBeans**: NetBeans is an open-source IDE that provides a user-friendly interface for Java development. It offers features like code templates, refactoring tools, and integrated support for various Java technologies.

- **Visual Studio Code (VS Code)**: VS Code is a lightweight, open-source code editor developed by Microsoft. It has a thriving ecosystem of extensions, including ones for Java development, making it a versatile choice for many developers.

Choose the code editor or IDE that suits your workflow and style. Whichever tool you select, you'll typically need to install the corresponding Java extensions or plugins to enhance your Java development experience.

Managing Dependencies with Build Tools

In Java development, you often need to manage external libraries and dependencies for your projects. Build tools like Apache Maven and Gradle simplify the process of handling dependencies, building projects, and managing project lifecycles.

- **Apache Maven**: Maven is a widely used build automation tool that uses XML configuration files (POM files) to define project settings and dependencies. It can automatically download and manage dependencies from central repositories.

- **Gradle**: Gradle is another popular build tool that allows you to define project configurations using a Groovy or Kotlin DSL. It offers flexibility and powerful dependency management capabilities.

To use Maven or Gradle, you need to create a project configuration file (e.g., `pom.xml` for Maven or `build.gradle` for Gradle) and specify your project's dependencies. These build tools will then handle the downloading and management of the required libraries.

Setting up your Java development environment is the first step toward writing Java code efficiently. Once you've completed these setup steps, you'll be ready to start creating Java applications, exploring libraries, and building software that leverages Java's capabilities. In the following chapters, we'll delve deeper into Java's features and best practices.

1.4 Your First Java Program

In this section, we will guide you through creating your very first Java program. We'll break down the essential components of a Java program and show you how to compile and run it. By the end of this section, you'll have written and executed your "Hello, World!" program in Java.

A Java program consists of several elements. Let's take a look at the basic structure:

```java
public class HelloWorld {
    public static void main(String[] args) {
        // Your code goes here
        System.out.println("Hello, World!");
    }
}
```

Here's a breakdown of the key components:

- `public class HelloWorld`: This line defines a class named `HelloWorld`. In Java, every program starts with a class definition, and the class name must match the filename (e.g., `HelloWorld.java`).

- `public static void main(String[] args)`: This line declares the `main` method. The `main` method is the entry point of your Java program. It has a specific signature with the `public`, `static`, `void`, and `String[]` `args` parts, which we'll explain shortly.

- `// Your code goes here`: This is a comment line. Comments in Java are ignored by the compiler and are used to provide explanations and documentation for your code.

- `System.out.println("Hello, World!");`: This line is a statement that prints "Hello, World!" to the console. The `System.out.println` method is used for output in Java.

The main Method

The `main` method is a special method in Java, and it serves as the starting point of your program. Let's break down its components:

- `public`: This keyword indicates that the `main` method can be accessed from outside the class. It allows the Java runtime to call this method to start your program.

- `static`: The `static` keyword means that the `main` method belongs to the class itself, rather than to instances of the class. It allows you to call the `main` method without creating an object of the class.

- `void`: This is the return type of the `main` method. `void` means the method does not return any value.

- `String[] args`: This is the parameter list of the `main` method. It specifies an array of strings called `args`. This parameter allows you to pass command-line arguments to your program when you run it.

Now that you understand the basic structure of a Java program, let's compile and run it. Follow these steps:

1. Open a text editor or your preferred Java development environment.

2. Create a new file and save it with the name HelloWorld.java.

3. Copy the following code into HelloWorld.java:

```java
public class HelloWorld {
    public static void main(String[] args) {
        System.out.println("Hello, World!");
    }
}
```

4. Save the file.

5. Open your terminal or command prompt.

6. Navigate to the directory where HelloWorld.java is located using the cd command.

7. Compile the Java source code by running the following command:

```
javac HelloWorld.java
```

If there are no errors in your code, this command will generate a HelloWorld.class file.

8. Run your Java program with the following command:

```
java HelloWorld
```

You should see the output "Hello, World!" displayed in your terminal.

Congratulations! You've just written and executed your first Java program. This simple "Hello, World!" program is a fundamental starting point for learning Java, and you can build upon it as you explore the language's features and capabilities in the subsequent chapters.

1.5 Java Development Tools

In this section, we will explore some of the essential Java development tools that can enhance your productivity and streamline the software development process. Java offers a rich ecosystem of tools, both command-line and graphical, to help you write, test, debug, and manage Java applications.

1.5.1 Integrated Development Environments (IDEs)

Integrated Development Environments (IDEs) are powerful tools that provide a comprehensive environment for Java development. Here are a few popular Java IDEs:

Eclipse

Eclipse is a widely used open-source IDE known for its extensibility. It supports Java development out of the box and offers features like code completion, debugging, and project management. Eclipse also has a vast ecosystem of plugins that can enhance its functionality for various purposes.

IntelliJ IDEA

IntelliJ IDEA, developed by JetBrains, is a commercial IDE known for its intelligent code analysis and developer-friendly features. It offers a free Community Edition and a paid Ultimate Edition with advanced capabilities. IntelliJ IDEA provides excellent support for Java development and other JVM languages.

NetBeans

NetBeans is an open-source IDE that provides a user-friendly interface for Java development. It offers features like code templates, refactoring tools, and integrated support for Java technologies such as JavaServer Faces (JSF) and Java EE.

Visual Studio Code (VS Code)

Visual Studio Code is a lightweight, open-source code editor developed by Microsoft. It has gained popularity for its versatility and an extensive collection of extensions. You can turn VS Code into a powerful Java development environment by installing Java extensions, making it an attractive choice for many developers.

1.5.2 Build Tools

Build tools are essential for managing project dependencies, compiling code, running tests, and creating distributable packages. Two prominent build tools in the Java ecosystem are Apache Maven and Gradle.

Apache Maven

Maven is a widely used build automation tool that simplifies project management and dependency resolution. It uses XML-based project configuration files (POM files) to define project settings and dependencies. Maven can automatically download required libraries from central repositories, making it easy to manage dependencies.

Gradle

Gradle is another popular build tool that offers flexibility and powerful dependency management. It uses Groovy or Kotlin DSL for defining build configurations, making it highly customizable. Gradle is known for its performance and is widely adopted for Android app development.

1.5.3 Version Control Systems

Version control systems (VCS) are essential for tracking changes to your code, collaborating with others, and ensuring code integrity. Git is the most widely used VCS in the Java development community.

Git

Git is a distributed version control system known for its speed and flexibility. It allows you to track changes to your code, create branches for development and experimentation, and collaborate with other developers through platforms like GitHub and GitLab. Git is an indispensable tool for managing code in Java projects.

1.5.4 Testing Frameworks

Testing is a crucial part of software development, and Java offers several testing frameworks to help you write and run tests for your code.

JUnit

JUnit is a widely used testing framework for Java. It provides annotations and assertions for writing unit tests and automates test execution. JUnit is an essential tool for practicing Test-Driven Development (TDD) and ensuring the reliability of your Java code.

1.5.5 Integrated Development Environment (IDE) Plugins

IDEs often provide a range of plugins and extensions that can enhance your development experience. These plugins can include tools for code analysis, code generation, and integration with other development tools and frameworks. When using an IDE for Java development, explore its plugin ecosystem to find tools that suit your needs.

In this section, we've introduced you to some of the fundamental Java development tools that can help you write, test, and manage your Java applications more effectively. Depending on your project's requirements and your personal preferences, you may choose different combinations of these tools to create a development environment that suits your needs. As you dive deeper into Java development, you'll discover additional tools and libraries that can further enhance your productivity and help you build robust Java applications.

Chapter 2: Understanding Java Basics

2.1 Variables and Data Types

In Java, variables are fundamental elements used for storing and managing data. To work effectively in Java, it's crucial to understand the various data types available and how to declare and use variables. In this section, we'll explore Java's data types, variable declaration, and common conventions.

Data Types in Java

Java supports several built-in data types, each designed to hold specific types of data. These data types can be broadly categorized into two groups: primitive data types and reference data types.

Primitive Data Types

Primitive data types represent simple values and are stored directly in memory. There are eight primitive data types in Java:

1. **byte**: 8-bit integer data type.
2. **short**: 16-bit integer data type.
3. **int**: 32-bit integer data type.
4. **long**: 64-bit integer data type.
5. **float**: 32-bit floating-point data type.
6. **double**: 64-bit floating-point data type.
7. **char**: 16-bit character data type.
8. **boolean**: Represents true or false values.

Each primitive data type has a default value, which is the initial value assigned to a variable of that type if no other value is explicitly provided.

Reference Data Types

Reference data types are used to refer to objects or complex data structures. These data types do not store the actual data but instead store references (memory addresses) to the objects. Some common reference data types include:

- **String**: Represents a sequence of characters.
- **Arrays**: Ordered collections of elements of the same type.
- **Classes**: User-defined data types created using classes and objects.

Variable Declaration

To declare a variable in Java, you specify the data type followed by the variable's name. Here's the general syntax for declaring variables:

```
data_type variable_name;
```

For example, to declare an integer variable named myNumber, you would write:

```
int myNumber;
```

You can also assign an initial value when declaring a variable:

```
int myNumber = 42;
```

Variable Naming Conventions

When naming variables in Java, it's essential to follow naming conventions to write clean and readable code. Here are some common naming conventions:

- Variable names should start with a letter (a-z or A-Z) or an underscore (_) followed by letters, digits (0-9), or underscores.
- Variable names are case-sensitive, so myVar and myvar are considered different variables.
- Use meaningful names that describe the variable's purpose, like totalScore instead of ts or x.

Constants

In Java, you can define constants using the final keyword. Constants are variables whose values cannot be changed once assigned. Here's how you define a constant:

```
final int MAX_VALUE = 100;
```

Type Casting

In some cases, you may need to convert a value from one data type to another. This process is called type casting. There are two types of type casting in Java: implicit and explicit.

- Implicit casting (widening): Java automatically converts a smaller data type to a larger data type without the need for explicit casting. For example, you can assign an int to a double without issues.

```
int num = 42;
double numDouble = num; // Implicit casting
```

- Explicit casting (narrowing): When you need to convert a larger data type to a smaller data type, you must use explicit casting. This can result in data loss if the value is too large for the smaller data type.

```
double numDouble = 42.0;
int numInt = (int) numDouble; // Explicit casting
```

Understanding data types, variable declaration, and naming conventions is fundamental to Java programming. These concepts lay the foundation for writing code that can efficiently store and manipulate data, making it essential to grasp as you progress in your Java journey. In the subsequent sections, we'll delve deeper into Java's basic constructs and explore how to use them effectively in your programs.

2.2 Operators in Java

Operators in Java are symbols or special keywords that perform specific operations on one or more operands. These operations can range from basic arithmetic calculations to complex logical evaluations. Understanding and using operators is fundamental to writing Java code. In this section, we'll explore various types of operators in Java.

Arithmetic Operators

Arithmetic operators are used for basic mathematical operations. Java provides the following arithmetic operators:

- **Addition (+)**: Adds two operands.
- **Subtraction (-)**: Subtracts the right operand from the left operand.
- **Multiplication (*)**: Multiplies two operands.
- **Division (/)**: Divides the left operand by the right operand.
- **Modulus (%)**: Returns the remainder of the division of the left operand by the right operand.

Here's an example of using arithmetic operators:

```
int a = 10;
int b = 3;

int sum = a + b;        // 13
int difference = a - b; // 7
int product = a * b;    // 30
int quotient = a / b;   // 3
int remainder = a % b;  // 1
```

Assignment Operators

Assignment operators are used to assign values to variables. The most basic assignment operator is the equals sign (=), which assigns the value on the right-hand side to the variable on the left-hand side.

```
int x = 5; // Assigns the value 5 to the variable x
```

Java also provides shorthand assignment operators that combine arithmetic operations with assignment. For example, the += operator adds the right operand to the left operand and assigns the result to the left operand.

```
int y = 10;
y += 3; // Equivalent to y = y + 3; y is now 13
```

Comparison Operators

Comparison operators are used to compare two values and return a boolean result (true or false). Java provides the following comparison operators:

- **Equal to (==)**: Checks if two values are equal.
- **Not equal to (!=)**: Checks if two values are not equal.
- **Greater than (>)**: Checks if the left operand is greater than the right operand.
- **Less than (<)**: Checks if the left operand is less than the right operand.
- **Greater than or equal to (>=)**: Checks if the left operand is greater than or equal to the right operand.
- **Less than or equal to (<=)**: Checks if the left operand is less than or equal to the right operand.

Here's an example of using comparison operators:

```
int p = 5;
int q = 10;

boolean isEqual = (p == q);   // false
boolean isNotEqual = (p != q); // true
boolean isGreater = (p > q);   // false
boolean isLess = (p < q);      // true
```

Logical Operators

Logical operators are used to perform logical operations on boolean values. Java provides the following logical operators:

- **Logical AND (&&)**: Returns true if both operands are true.
- **Logical OR (||)**: Returns true if at least one operand is true.
- **Logical NOT (!)**: Inverts the value of the operand (changes true to false and vice versa).

Here's an example of using logical operators:

```
boolean a = true;
boolean b = false;

boolean result1 = a && b; // false (true && false)
boolean result2 = a || b; // true (true || false)
boolean result3 = !a;     // false (!true)
```

Bitwise Operators

Bitwise operators perform operations on individual bits of integers. They are used in low-level programming and specific scenarios. Java provides the following bitwise operators:

- **Bitwise AND (&)**: Performs a bitwise AND operation.

- **Bitwise OR (|)**: Performs a bitwise OR operation.
- **Bitwise XOR (^)**: Performs a bitwise XOR (exclusive OR) operation.
- **Bitwise NOT (~)**: Inverts all bits.
- **Left Shift (<<)**: Shifts bits to the left.
- **Right Shift (>>)**: Shifts bits to the right with sign extension.
- **Unsigned Right Shift (>>>)**: Shifts bits to the right without sign extension.

Bitwise operators are mainly used in scenarios involving binary data manipulation, such as working with hardware interfaces or encryption.

```java
int x = 5;   // Binary: 0101
int y = 3;   // Binary: 0011

int bitwiseAnd = x & y; // Result: 0001 (1)
int bitwiseOr = x | y;  // Result: 0111 (7)
int bitwiseXor = x ^ y; // Result: 0110 (6)
int bitwiseNot = ~x;    // Result: 11111111111111111111111111111010 (-6)
int leftShift = x << 1; // Result: 1010 (10)
int rightShift = x >> 1; // Result: 0010 (2)
```

Conditional Operator (Ternary Operator)

The conditional operator, often referred to as the ternary operator, is a shorthand way to write simple if-else statements. It has the following syntax:

```java
condition ? expression_if_true : expression_if_false
```

Here's an example:

```java
int num1 = 5;
int num2 = 10;

int max = (num1 > num2) ? num1 : num2; // max is assigned the value 10
```

In this example, max is assigned the value of num1 if the condition (num1 > num2) is true, and it's assigned the value of num2 if the condition is false.

Understanding these operators is crucial for performing various operations and making decisions in your Java programs. Operators allow you to manipulate data, control program flow, and perform logical evaluations, making them indispensable tools in Java programming. In the following sections, we'll continue to explore more aspects of Java programming to deepen your understanding of the language.

2.3 Control Flow: Conditional Statements

Conditional statements in Java allow you to control the flow of your program based on certain conditions. Using these statements, you can make decisions, execute specific code blocks, and handle different scenarios. In this section, we'll explore the conditional statements in Java, including if, else if, else, and switch.

The if Statement

The if statement is used to execute a block of code if a specified condition is true. Here's the basic syntax of the if statement:

```java
if (condition) {
    // Code to execute if the condition is true
}
```

Here's an example:

```java
int x = 10;
if (x > 5) {
    System.out.println("x is greater than 5");
}
```

In this example, the code inside the if block is executed because the condition x > 5 is true.

The if-else Statement

The if-else statement allows you to execute one block of code if a condition is true and another block if the condition is false. Here's the syntax:

```java
if (condition) {
    // Code to execute if the condition is true
} else {
    // Code to execute if the condition is false
}
```

Example:

```java
int y = 3;
if (y > 5) {
    System.out.println("y is greater than 5");
} else {
    System.out.println("y is not greater than 5");
}
```

In this example, because y is not greater than 5, the code inside the else block is executed.

The else if Statement

The else if statement is used when you have multiple conditions to check. It allows you to specify additional conditions to test if the previous ones are false. Here's the syntax:

```java
if (condition1) {
    // Code to execute if condition1 is true
} else if (condition2) {
```

```
    // Code to execute if condition2 is true
} else {
    // Code to execute if none of the conditions are true
}
```

Example:

```
int z = 7;
if (z < 5) {
    System.out.println("z is less than 5");
} else if (z == 5) {
    System.out.println("z is equal to 5");
} else {
    System.out.println("z is greater than 5");
}
```

In this example, because z is greater than 5, the code inside the else block is executed.

The switch Statement

The switch statement is used to select one of many code blocks to be executed. It is often used when you have multiple cases to compare against a single value. Here's the syntax:

```
switch (expression) {
    case value1:
        // Code to execute if expression matches value1
        break;
    case value2:
        // Code to execute if expression matches value2
        break;
    // More cases...
    default:
        // Code to execute if no cases match
}
```

Example:

```
int dayOfWeek = 3;
String dayName;

switch (dayOfWeek) {
    case 1:
        dayName = "Monday";
        break;
    case 2:
        dayName = "Tuesday";
        break;
    case 3:
        dayName = "Wednesday";
        break;
    // More cases...
```

```
    default:
        dayName = "Invalid day";
}
```

In this example, the switch statement assigns the value "Wednesday" to the dayName variable because dayOfWeek is 3.

Conditional statements are crucial for controlling the logic and behavior of your Java programs. They allow you to make decisions, handle different scenarios, and create dynamic code that responds to changing conditions. In the next section, we'll explore loops, which are essential for repeating code execution in Java.

2.4 Control Flow: Loops

Loops are essential constructs in programming that allow you to execute a block of code repeatedly. Java provides several types of loops, each serving different purposes. In this section, we'll explore the three primary types of loops in Java: for, while, and do-while.

The for Loop

The for loop is commonly used when you know the exact number of iterations you want to perform. It consists of three parts: initialization, condition, and iteration expression. Here's the syntax:

```
for (initialization; condition; iteration_expression) {
    // Code to execute in each iteration
}
```

Example:

```
for (int i = 1; i <= 5; i++) {
    System.out.println("Iteration " + i);
}
```

In this example, the for loop iterates five times, printing "Iteration 1" to "Iteration 5."

The while Loop

The while loop is used when you want to repeat a block of code as long as a certain condition is true. It has the following syntax:

```
while (condition) {
    // Code to execute as long as the condition is true
}
```

Example:

```
int count = 1;
while (count <= 5) {
```

```java
    System.out.println("Iteration " + count);
    count++;
}
```

In this example, the while loop continues to iterate as long as count is less than or equal to 5.

The do-while Loop

The do-while loop is similar to the while loop, but it guarantees that the block of code is executed at least once, even if the condition is initially false. Here's the syntax:

```java
do {
    // Code to execute at least once
} while (condition);
```

Example:

```java
int num = 1;
do {
    System.out.println("Value of num: " + num);
    num++;
} while (num <= 5);
```

In this example, the code block is executed once, and then the condition is checked. If the condition is true, the loop continues to execute.

Loop Control Statements

Java provides several loop control statements that allow you to control the flow of loops:

- **break**: It terminates the loop and transfers control to the statement immediately after the loop.

Example:

```java
for (int i = 1; i <= 10; i++) {
    if (i == 5) {
        break; // Terminate the loop when i is 5
    }
    System.out.println("Value of i: " + i);
}
```

- **continue**: It skips the current iteration and continues with the next iteration of the loop.

Example:

```java
for (int i = 1; i <= 5; i++) {
    if (i == 3) {
        continue; // Skip iteration 3
    }
```

```
        System.out.println("Value of i: " + i);
}
```

- **return**: In methods, it can be used to exit the method and return a value to the caller. It is not specific to loops but can be used to exit a loop if the loop is inside a method.

Loop control statements provide flexibility and fine-grained control over loop execution.

Infinite Loops

Be cautious when using loops, as improper loop conditions can lead to infinite loops, which continue executing indefinitely. Infinite loops can hang your program, causing it to become unresponsive. To prevent this, ensure that the loop condition eventually becomes false or include a mechanism, such as a loop control statement, to exit the loop.

Loops are fundamental for performing repetitive tasks and iterating over collections of data in Java. They enable you to write efficient and concise code for a wide range of applications. In the next section, we'll explore arrays and collections, which are commonly used to store and manipulate data in Java programs.

2.5 Arrays and Collections

In Java, arrays and collections are data structures that allow you to store multiple values of the same or different data types. They are essential for organizing and working with data efficiently. In this section, we'll explore arrays and collections, including arrays, ArrayLists, and the Java Collections Framework.

Arrays

An array is a fixed-size, ordered collection of elements of the same data type. In Java, arrays are declared with a specific size, and that size cannot be changed once the array is created. Here's how you declare an array:

```
dataType[] arrayName = new dataType[size];
```

Example:

```
int[] numbers = new int[5]; // Declares an integer array of size 5
```

You can initialize an array with values during declaration or assign values later:

```
int[] scores = {95, 88, 72, 100, 90}; // Initializing with values

// Assigning values later
numbers[0] = 42;
numbers[1] = 55;
// ...
```

Arrays are indexed starting from 0. You access elements using square brackets and the index:

```
int firstNumber = numbers[0]; // Accesses the first element (index 0)
```

Arrays are useful when you know the size of your data in advance and need direct access to elements by index.

ArrayLists

An `ArrayList` is part of the Java Collections Framework and provides a dynamic, resizable array-like data structure. Unlike arrays, `ArrayLists` can grow or shrink as needed. Here's how you create an `ArrayList`:

```
import java.util.ArrayList;

ArrayList<dataType> listName = new ArrayList<>();
```

Example:

```
import java.util.ArrayList;

ArrayList<String> names = new ArrayList<>();
```

You can add elements to an `ArrayList` using the add method:

```
names.add("Alice");
names.add("Bob");
names.add("Charlie");
```

You can access elements using the get method, which takes an index:

```
String firstName = names.get(0); // Accesses the first element
```

`ArrayLists` are versatile and convenient when you need a dynamic data structure that can change in size during runtime.

The Java Collections Framework

The Java Collections Framework provides a comprehensive set of classes and interfaces for working with collections of objects. It includes data structures like `ArrayList`, `LinkedList`, `HashSet`, `HashMap`, and more. These collections offer various features such as dynamic sizing, sorting, and efficient retrieval.

Here's an example of using the `ArrayList` class from the Collections Framework:

```
import java.util.ArrayList;

ArrayList<Integer> numbers = new ArrayList<>();
numbers.add(10);
numbers.add(20);
numbers.add(30);
```

```
int sum = 0;
for (int num : numbers) {
    sum += num;
}
System.out.println("Sum: " + sum);
```

In this example, we use an `ArrayList` to store integers and calculate their sum using an enhanced for loop.

Common Operations on Collections

Collections in Java provide a wide range of operations, including adding and removing elements, searching, sorting, and more. Here are some common operations:

- Adding elements: Use the add method to insert elements.
- Removing elements: Use the `remove` method to delete elements.
- Checking if an element exists: Use the `contains` method to check for element existence.
- Iterating through elements: Use loops like `for-each` to traverse elements.
- Sorting: Use the `Collections.sort()` method for sorting collections.

```
import java.util.ArrayList;
import java.util.Collections;

ArrayList<String> fruits = new ArrayList<>();
fruits.add("Apple");
fruits.add("Banana");
fruits.add("Cherry");

Collections.sort(fruits); // Sorts the ArrayList alphabetically
```

Arrays and collections are fundamental for managing and manipulating data in Java. Depending on your requirements, you can choose between fixed-size arrays for predictable sizes or dynamic collections like `ArrayList` for flexibility. In the next sections, we'll delve into more advanced Java concepts, including object-oriented programming and the Java Standard Library.

Chapter 3: Object-Oriented Programming in Java

3.1 Classes and Objects

Object-oriented programming (OOP) is a programming paradigm that revolves around the concept of objects, which are instances of classes. In Java, OOP is a fundamental approach to structuring and organizing code. In this section, we'll explore the concepts of classes and objects in Java and understand how they are used to model real-world entities and their behaviors.

Classes in Java

A class is a blueprint or template for creating objects. It defines the structure and behavior that its objects will have. In Java, a class is declared using the class keyword followed by the class name. Here's a simple class definition:

```java
public class Car {
    // Fields (attributes)
    String make;
    String model;
    int year;

    // Methods (behaviors)
    void start() {
        System.out.println("The car is starting.");
    }

    void stop() {
        System.out.println("The car is stopping.");
    }
}
```

In this example, we've defined a Car class with fields (attributes) for make, model, and year, as well as methods (behaviors) for start and stop.

Objects in Java

An object is an instance of a class. You can create multiple objects (instances) from a single class blueprint. To create an object in Java, you use the new keyword followed by the class constructor. Here's how you create instances of the Car class:

```java
Car car1 = new Car();
Car car2 = new Car();
```

In this code, car1 and car2 are two distinct objects of the Car class.

Accessing Fields and Methods

Once you have objects, you can access their fields (attributes) and methods using the dot notation. For example, to set the make field of car1, you can do the following:

```
car1.make = "Toyota";
```

To call the start method of car2, you can do the following:

```
car2.start();
```

Constructors

Constructors are special methods used to initialize objects when they are created. If you don't provide a constructor in your class, Java will provide a default constructor with no arguments. However, you can define your own constructors with custom initialization logic. Here's an example of a constructor in the Car class:

```java
public class Car {
    String make;
    String model;
    int year;

    // Constructor
    public Car(String make, String model, int year) {
        this.make = make;
        this.model = model;
        this.year = year;
    }

    // Methods
    void start() {
        System.out.println("The car is starting.");
    }

    void stop() {
        System.out.println("The car is stopping.");
    }
}
```

In this modified Car class, we've added a constructor that takes parameters for make, model, and year and initializes the corresponding fields.

The this Keyword

The this keyword refers to the current instance of the class. It is often used to distinguish between instance variables and parameters with the same name in constructors and methods. In the constructor example above, we used this to access the instance variables and assign values to them.

```java
        this.make = make;
        this.model = model;
        this.year = year;
```

Encapsulation

Encapsulation is one of the core principles of OOP, and it involves bundling the data (fields) and methods (behaviors) that operate on the data into a single unit, known as a class. In Java, you can control the access to class members (fields and methods) using access modifiers like `public`, `private`, and `protected`. This helps ensure data integrity and provides encapsulation.

```java
public class Car {
    private String make;
    private String model;
    private int year;

    // Constructor and methods...

    // Getter method for make
    public String getMake() {
        return make;
    }

    // Setter method for make
    public void setMake(String make) {
        this.make = make;
    }
}
```

In this example, we've made the `make` field `private` and provided getter and setter methods to access and modify it.

Object-Oriented Concepts

Java's support for OOP includes key concepts like inheritance, polymorphism, and abstraction, which allow you to build complex and modular software systems. Inheritance enables you to create new classes based on existing ones, inheriting their fields and methods. Polymorphism allows objects of different classes to be treated as objects of a common superclass. Abstraction allows you to define the essential characteristics of an object while hiding unnecessary details.

Understanding classes and objects is the foundation of object-oriented programming in Java. It enables you to model real-world entities as classes, create instances of those classes as objects, and define their behavior through methods. In the following sections, we'll delve deeper into advanced OOP concepts and explore topics like inheritance, encapsulation, and interfaces.

3.2 Inheritance and Polymorphism

Inheritance and polymorphism are fundamental concepts in object-oriented programming (OOP) that enable code reuse, extensibility, and flexibility in Java. In this section, we'll explore these concepts in detail.

Inheritance

Inheritance is the mechanism in OOP that allows a new class to be based on an existing class, inheriting its properties and behaviors. The existing class is known as the superclass or parent class, and the new class is called the subclass or child class. In Java, you can achieve inheritance using the extends keyword. Here's a simple example:

```java
// Superclass (parent class)
class Vehicle {
    void start() {
        System.out.println("Vehicle is starting.");
    }

    void stop() {
        System.out.println("Vehicle is stopping.");
    }
}

// Subclass (child class)
class Car extends Vehicle {
    void accelerate() {
        System.out.println("Car is accelerating.");
    }

    void brake() {
        System.out.println("Car is braking.");
    }
}
```

In this example, the Car class inherits from the Vehicle class. This means that the Car class has access to the start and stop methods defined in the Vehicle class, in addition to its own accelerate and brake methods.

Polymorphism

Polymorphism is another important OOP concept that allows objects of different classes to be treated as objects of a common superclass. This enables flexibility and code reusability. In Java, polymorphism is achieved through method overriding and interfaces.

Method overriding occurs when a subclass provides a specific implementation of a method that is already defined in its superclass. To override a method, you use the `@Override` annotation to indicate that you intend to provide a new implementation for a method inherited from the superclass. Here's an example:

```java
class Animal {
    void makeSound() {
        System.out.println("Animal makes a sound.");
    }
}

class Dog extends Animal {
    @Override
    void makeSound() {
        System.out.println("Dog barks.");
    }
}

class Cat extends Animal {
    @Override
    void makeSound() {
        System.out.println("Cat meows.");
    }
}
```

In this example, both the `Dog` and `Cat` classes override the `makeSound` method from the `Animal` class with their own implementations. When you create objects of these classes and call the `makeSound` method, the appropriate implementation is invoked based on the object's actual type.

```java
Animal myDog = new Dog();
Animal myCat = new Cat();

myDog.makeSound(); // Output: Dog barks.
myCat.makeSound(); // Output: Cat meows.
```

Polymorphism allows you to work with objects in a more generic way, treating them based on their common superclass, which can simplify code and make it more flexible.

Interfaces

In addition to method overriding, Java supports polymorphism through interfaces. An interface defines a contract of methods that a class must implement. A class can implement multiple interfaces, enabling it to exhibit different behaviors based on the interfaces it implements. Here's an example:

```java
// Interface
interface Shape {
```

```java
    double area();
}

// Classes implementing the Shape interface
class Circle implements Shape {
    double radius;

    Circle(double radius) {
        this.radius = radius;
    }

    @Override
    public double area() {
        return Math.PI * radius * radius;
    }
}

class Rectangle implements Shape {
    double width;
    double height;

    Rectangle(double width, double height) {
        this.width = width;
        this.height = height;
    }

    @Override
    public double area() {
        return width * height;
    }
}
```

In this example, both the `Circle` and `Rectangle` classes implement the `Shape` interface, which requires them to provide an implementation for the `area` method. This allows you to work with different shapes in a uniform way:

```java
Shape myCircle = new Circle(5.0);
Shape myRectangle = new Rectangle(4.0, 6.0);

double circleArea = myCircle.area();          // Calculate circle's area
double rectangleArea = myRectangle.area();    // Calculate rectangle's area
```

Polymorphism through interfaces enables you to create more versatile and modular code by defining common behavior that can be shared across classes.

Inheritance and polymorphism are powerful concepts in Java's object-oriented programming model. They enable code reuse, extensibility, and flexibility, making it easier to design and maintain complex software systems. In the next sections, we'll explore more OOP concepts, such as encapsulation, abstraction, and access modifiers.

3.3 Encapsulation and Access Modifiers

Encapsulation is one of the four fundamental object-oriented programming (OOP) concepts, alongside inheritance, polymorphism, and abstraction. It involves bundling the data (fields) and methods (behaviors) that operate on the data into a single unit, known as a class. In Java, access modifiers play a crucial role in achieving encapsulation by controlling the visibility and accessibility of class members (fields and methods). In this section, we'll explore encapsulation and the various access modifiers available in Java.

Encapsulation

Encapsulation is the practice of hiding the internal details and state of an object while exposing a well-defined interface to interact with the object. It promotes data integrity and prevents unauthorized access to or modification of an object's internal state. Encapsulation allows you to encapsulate the implementation details within a class and provide controlled access to class members.

Access Modifiers

Access modifiers are keywords in Java that determine the visibility and accessibility of class members (fields, methods, and nested classes). Java provides four main access modifiers:

1. **public**: Members marked as public are accessible from anywhere in the same project, including outside the package and even in different projects. This is the least restrictive access modifier.

2. **private**: Members marked as private are only accessible within the same class. They are not visible or accessible outside the class.

3. **protected**: Members marked as protected are accessible within the same class, within subclasses (even if they are in different packages), and within the same package. However, they are not accessible from outside the package if they are not part of a subclass.

4. **default (package-private)**: If a member has no access modifier specified (i.e., it is not explicitly marked as public, private, or protected), it is considered package-private. It is accessible within the same package but not outside the package.

Here's a visual representation of the accessibility levels from most accessible to least accessible:

*   public > protected > package-private (default) > private

Using Access Modifiers

You can apply access modifiers to class members to control their visibility. For example, consider a Car class:

```java
public class Car {
    private String make; // private field
    private String model; // private field

    public Car(String make, String model) {
        this.make = make;
        this.model = model;
    }

    public void start() { // public method
        System.out.println("Starting the car.");
    }

    protected void accelerate() { // protected method
        System.out.println("Accelerating the car.");
    }

    void stop() { // package-private method (default)
        System.out.println("Stopping the car.");
    }
}
```

In this example, make and model are private fields, start is a public method, accelerate is a protected method, and stop is a package-private (default) method.

Benefits of Encapsulation and Access Modifiers

1. **Data Hiding**: Encapsulation allows you to hide the internal state of an object, preventing unauthorized access and modification. This enhances data security and integrity.

2. **Controlled Access**: Access modifiers provide fine-grained control over the visibility of class members. You can determine which parts of your class are exposed to other classes and which remain hidden.

3. **Code Maintenance**: Encapsulation makes it easier to modify the internal implementation of a class without affecting other parts of the code that use the class. It promotes modular and maintainable code.

4. **Abstraction**: Encapsulation allows you to abstract the essential characteristics and behaviors of an object while hiding the implementation details. This simplifies the interaction with objects.

Best Practices

When using encapsulation and access modifiers in Java, consider the following best practices:

- Make fields `private` by default and provide getter and setter methods (public or protected) to access and modify the fields when necessary. This encapsulates the data and provides controlled access.

- Avoid exposing fields directly through public access. Instead, use getter and setter methods to enforce data validation and maintain control over data integrity.

- Use `protected` access when you want to provide visibility to subclasses, but be cautious about the potential impacts on class hierarchies and maintainability.

- Minimize the use of package-private (default) access unless it is necessary for class collaboration within the same package.

Encapsulation and access modifiers are crucial aspects of writing robust and maintainable Java code. They help manage complexity, improve code organization, and enhance security by controlling access to class members. Properly encapsulated classes provide clear and controlled interfaces for interacting with objects, making your code more reliable and easier to maintain.

3.4 Abstract Classes and Interfaces

Abstract classes and interfaces are essential components of Java's object-oriented programming (OOP) model, allowing you to define blueprints for classes and provide common behavior for multiple classes. In this section, we'll explore abstract classes and interfaces, their differences, and how to use them effectively.

Abstract Classes

An abstract class in Java is a class that cannot be instantiated directly; it serves as a blueprint for other classes. Abstract classes can contain abstract methods (methods without implementations) and concrete methods (methods with implementations). To define an abstract class, use the `abstract` keyword before the class declaration. Here's an example:

```java
abstract class Shape {
    abstract double area(); // Abstract method
    void printInfo() {
        System.out.println("This is a shape.");
    }
}
```

In this example, the `Shape` class is abstract, and it defines an abstract method `area()` that must be implemented by any concrete subclass. It also includes a concrete method `printInfo()` with an implementation.

Abstract Methods

Abstract methods are methods declared in an abstract class without providing an implementation. Concrete subclasses of the abstract class must provide implementations for these methods. Abstract methods are declared using the `abstract` keyword, and they end with a semicolon instead of a method body. Here's an example:

```java
abstract class Animal {
    abstract void makeSound(); // Abstract method
}

class Dog extends Animal {
    @Override
    void makeSound() {
        System.out.println("Dog barks.");
    }
}

class Cat extends Animal {
    @Override
    void makeSound() {
        System.out.println("Cat meows.");
    }
}
```

In this example, the `Animal` class defines an abstract method `makeSound()`, which is implemented by the `Dog` and `Cat` subclasses.

Concrete Methods

Abstract classes can also contain concrete methods, which have implementations. Subclasses can inherit and use these concrete methods without being forced to provide their implementations. This allows you to share common behavior among multiple classes. Here's an example:

```java
abstract class Vehicle {
    void start() {
        System.out.println("Vehicle is starting.");
    }

    abstract void stop();
}

class Car extends Vehicle {
    @Override
    void stop() {
        System.out.println("Car is stopping.");
    }
}
```

In this example, the `Vehicle` class includes a concrete method `start()` and an abstract method `stop()`. The `Car` class inherits the `start()` method and provides its implementation for the `stop()` method.

Interfaces

Interfaces are another way to define abstract blueprints in Java. Unlike abstract classes, interfaces can't contain concrete methods with implementations; they define a contract that classes must adhere to by implementing the interface's methods. To define an interface, use the `interface` keyword. Here's an example:

```java
interface Drawable {
    void draw(); // Abstract method
}
```

In this example, the `Drawable` interface defines an abstract method `draw()` that classes implementing the interface must provide.

Implementing Interfaces

A class can implement one or more interfaces by providing implementations for all the methods declared in those interfaces. To indicate that a class implements an interface, use the `implements` keyword. Here's an example:

```java
class Circle implements Drawable {
    double radius;

    Circle(double radius) {
        this.radius = radius;
    }

    @Override
    public void draw() {
        System.out.println("Drawing a circle with radius " + radius);
    }
}
```

In this example, the `Circle` class implements the `Drawable` interface and provides an implementation for the `draw()` method.

Abstract Classes vs. Interfaces

When deciding whether to use an abstract class or an interface, consider the following guidelines:

- Use an abstract class when you want to provide a common base class with some shared implementation details among its subclasses. Abstract classes can have fields, constructors, and concrete methods.

- Use an interface when you want to define a contract for multiple classes to implement, ensuring they have specific methods. Interfaces are suitable for defining shared behavior across unrelated classes.

- Java allows a class to extend one abstract class but implement multiple interfaces, providing flexibility in designing your class hierarchy.

- If you need to add new methods in the future but don't want to break existing subclasses, use an abstract class with a default implementation for the new method. Interfaces can't provide default implementations until Java 8 (with the introduction of default methods).

Abstract classes and interfaces are powerful tools in Java for defining blueprints and promoting code reusability and flexibility. By understanding when to use each, you can design robust and extensible class hierarchies in your Java applications.

3.5 Exception Handling

Exception handling is a crucial aspect of writing reliable and robust Java programs. In Java, exceptions are unexpected events or errors that can occur during the execution of a program. Exception handling allows you to gracefully handle these errors and prevent the program from crashing. In this section, we'll explore exception handling in Java, including how to handle exceptions and create custom exceptions.

The Exception Hierarchy

In Java, exceptions are organized into a hierarchy with the Throwable class at the top. There are two main types of exceptions: checked exceptions and unchecked exceptions (also known as runtime exceptions).

- **Checked Exceptions**: These are exceptions that the compiler requires you to handle explicitly, either by using a try-catch block or by declaring that the method throws the exception using the throws keyword. Examples include IOException and SQLException.

- **Unchecked Exceptions (Runtime Exceptions)**: These are exceptions that the compiler doesn't require you to handle explicitly. They usually represent programming errors or logic errors and extend the RuntimeException class. Examples include NullPointerException and ArrayIndexOutOfBoundsException.

Handling Exceptions with try-catch

You can handle exceptions using a try-catch block. The try block contains the code that might throw an exception, and the catch block catches and handles the exception. Here's an example:

```
try {
    // Code that may throw an exception
    int result = divide(10, 0);
    System.out.println("Result: " + result);
} catch (ArithmeticException e) {
    // Handle the exception
    System.err.println("An arithmetic error occurred: " + e.getMessage());
}
```

In this example, the divide method may throw an ArithmeticException if you attempt to divide by zero. The catch block catches the exception, and you can handle it by printing an error message.

The finally Block

You can also use a finally block along with a try-catch block. The code in the finally block executes regardless of whether an exception was thrown or not. It's typically used for cleanup tasks like closing files or releasing resources.

```
try {
    // Code that may throw an exception
} catch (Exception e) {
    // Handle the exception
} finally {
    // Cleanup code (always executed)
}
```

Throwing Exceptions

You can throw exceptions explicitly using the throw keyword. This is useful when you want to create custom exceptions or when a specific condition should lead to an exception.

```
if (condition) {
    throw new CustomException("This is a custom exception.");
}
```

Creating Custom Exceptions

You can create your own custom exceptions by extending the Exception class or one of its subclasses. This allows you to define application-specific exceptions that make error handling more meaningful.

```
class CustomException extends Exception {
    public CustomException(String message) {
        super(message);
    }
}
```

The throws Keyword

When defining a method that might throw a checked exception, you can use the throws keyword to declare the exception. This informs the caller that they need to handle or propagate the exception.

```java
public void readFile() throws IOException {
    // Code that reads a file and may throw IOException
}
```

Exception Propagation

If a method throws a checked exception and it's not caught within the method, the method must declare the exception using the throws keyword. This propagates the exception up the call stack until it is caught or until it reaches the top-level error handler.

Best Practices for Exception Handling

Here are some best practices for exception handling in Java:

1. Catch only the exceptions you can handle: Avoid catching exceptions that you can't handle effectively. Let higher-level methods or the top-level error handler deal with them.

2. Use meaningful error messages: When creating custom exceptions or handling exceptions, provide clear and meaningful error messages. This helps with debugging and makes error messages more informative.

3. Use multiple catch blocks when necessary: If you need to handle different types of exceptions differently, use multiple catch blocks, each for a specific exception type.

4. Log exceptions: Logging exceptions is essential for diagnosing issues in production. Use a logging framework to log exceptions with appropriate levels (e.g., ERROR or WARN).

5. Avoid using exceptions for control flow: Exceptions should not be used as a part of regular program logic. They are meant for handling exceptional conditions.

Exception handling is an essential part of writing reliable and robust Java applications. It allows you to gracefully handle errors and unexpected situations, ensuring that your program continues to run smoothly even when problems occur. By following best practices and using exception handling effectively, you can create more reliable and maintainable Java code.

Chapter 4: Java Standard Library

4.1 Introduction to the Java Standard Library

The Java Standard Library, often referred to as the Java Standard API (Application Programming Interface), is a vast collection of classes and packages that provide essential functionality for Java applications. These classes cover a wide range of areas, from basic data manipulation to advanced topics like networking and database access. In this section, we'll introduce you to the Java Standard Library and some of its key packages and classes.

Packages in the Java Standard Library

The Java Standard Library is organized into packages, each containing related classes and interfaces. Some of the core packages in the Java Standard Library include:

- **java.lang**: This package contains fundamental classes and objects that are automatically imported into every Java program. It includes classes like String, Object, and exceptions like NullPointerException.

- **java.util**: The java.util package provides data structures and utility classes, including collections (e.g., List, Set, Map), date and time utilities (Date, Calendar), and the Scanner class for input.

- **java.io**: This package is essential for handling input and output operations. It includes classes for reading and writing files, streams, and readers/writers for character-based input/output.

- **java.net**: The java.net package offers classes for network programming. It includes classes for creating network sockets, handling URLs, and making HTTP requests.

- **java.sql**: For database connectivity and SQL operations, the java.sql package provides classes like Connection, Statement, and ResultSet for interacting with relational databases.

- **java.awt and javax.swing**: These packages are part of Java's Abstract Window Toolkit (AWT) and Swing libraries, respectively, and are used for creating graphical user interfaces (GUIs).

Importing Classes and Packages

To use classes and packages from the Java Standard Library in your Java program, you need to import them using the import statement. For example:

```
import java.util.ArrayList;
import java.util.List;
import java.io.IOException;
```

You can also use the wildcard * to import all classes and interfaces within a package:

```
import java.util.*;
```

Here are some commonly used classes and methods from the Java Standard Library:

- `String` class: Used for manipulating and working with strings. It provides various methods for string manipulation, such as `substring()`, `length()`, and `charAt()`.

- `ArrayList` class: A dynamic array-based data structure that's part of the Java Collections Framework. It allows you to create resizable lists of objects.

- `File` class: Part of the `java.io` package, this class represents files and directories on the file system. It provides methods for file and directory manipulation, such as `createNewFile()`, `delete()`, and `listFiles()`.

- `Date` class: Provides date and time functionality. It is commonly used to work with timestamps and date-related calculations.

- `Scanner` class: Used for reading user input from the console or parsing text files. It simplifies input handling by providing methods like `next()`, `nextInt()`, and `nextLine()`.

- `URLConnection` class: Part of the `java.net` package, it's used for opening a connection to a URL and reading from or writing to it. It's useful for making HTTP requests and accessing web resources.

These are just a few examples of the classes and packages available in the Java Standard Library. The library is extensive and covers a wide array of functionality, making it a valuable resource for Java developers. In the following sections, we'll delve deeper into some of the key packages and explore specific topics and features provided by the Java Standard Library.

4.2 Working with Strings

Strings are a fundamental data type in Java, and working with them is a common task in programming. In this section, we'll explore various operations and methods for working with strings in the Java Standard Library.

Creating Strings

You can create strings in Java using either string literals or by using the `String` class constructor. Here are some examples:

```
String str1 = "Hello, World!"; // Using a string literal
String str2 = new String("Java"); // Using the constructor
```

String Concatenation

Concatenating strings in Java is straightforward. You can use the + operator to combine two or more strings:

```java
String firstName = "John";
String lastName = "Doe";
String fullName = firstName + " " + lastName; // Concatenate first and last names
```

String Length

To get the length (number of characters) of a string, you can use the `length()` method:

```java
String text = "This is a sample text.";
int length = text.length(); // Get the length of the string
```

Accessing Characters in a String

You can access individual characters in a string using the `charAt()` method. The index of the first character is 0:

```java
String str = "Java";
char firstChar = str.charAt(0); // Get the first character ('J')
char secondChar = str.charAt(1); // Get the second character ('a')
```

Substrings

To extract a portion of a string, you can use the `substring()` method. It takes either a starting index or a starting and ending index:

```java
String text = "Hello, World!";
String substring1 = text.substring(7); // Get substring from index 7 to the end ("World!")
String substring2 = text.substring(0, 5); // Get substring from index 0 to 5 ("Hello")
```

Searching in Strings

You can search for specific substrings within a string using methods like `indexOf()` and `contains()`:

```java
String text = "The quick brown fox jumps over the lazy dog.";
int indexOfFox = text.indexOf("fox"); // Find the index of "fox" (position 16)
boolean containsDog = text.contains("dog"); // Check if the string contains "dog" (true)
```

Modifying Strings

Strings in Java are immutable, which means you cannot change their content once created. When you perform operations that modify a string, a new string is created. Here's an example of concatenating strings:

```
String original = "Hello, ";
String modified = original + "World!"; // Creates a new string
```

String Comparison

To compare strings for equality, you should use the equals() method, which compares the content of the strings. Using == compares references:

```
String str1 = "Java";
String str2 = "Java";
boolean isEqual = str1.equals(str2); // Check if the strings are equal (true)
boolean isSameReference = str1 == str2; // Check if the references are the sa
me (true)
```

String Manipulation

The String class provides various methods for manipulating strings, including changing case, trimming whitespace, and replacing substrings. Here are some examples:

```
String text = "   Hello, World!   ";
String trimmedText = text.trim(); // Remove leading and trailing whitespace
String upperCaseText = text.toUpperCase(); // Convert to uppercase
String replacedText = text.replace("World", "Universe"); // Replace "World" w
ith "Universe"
```

StringBuilder and StringBuffer

If you need to perform a lot of string concatenation or modification operations, it's more efficient to use StringBuilder (or StringBuffer for thread-safe operations) instead of repeatedly creating new strings. These classes provide mutable sequences of characters:

```
StringBuilder builder = new StringBuilder();
builder.append("Hello, ");
builder.append("Java");
String result = builder.toString(); // Convert StringBuilder to a String
```

String Formatting

Java provides the String.format() method for formatting strings using placeholders and format specifiers. Here's an example of formatting a date:

```
import java.text.SimpleDateFormat;
import java.util.Date;

Date currentDate = new Date();
```

```java
String formattedDate = String.format("Today is %tA, %<td %<tB %<tY", currentD
ate);
```

Regular Expressions

The Java Standard Library includes the `java.util.regex` package for working with regular expressions. You can use regular expressions for advanced string manipulation tasks, such as pattern matching and substitution.

```java
import java.util.regex.*;

String text = "The quick brown fox jumps over the lazy dog.";
Pattern pattern = Pattern.compile("fox");
Matcher matcher = pattern.matcher(text);
boolean found = matcher.find(); // Check if the pattern is found
```

Working with strings is a fundamental part of Java programming. By understanding and

4.3 File I/O in Java

File Input/Output (I/O) operations are essential for working with files and data on disk in Java applications. In this section, we'll explore how to perform file I/O operations using the Java Standard Library.

Reading Files

To read data from a file in Java, you can use classes like `File`, `FileInputStream`, `BufferedReader`, and `Scanner`. Here's a basic example using `BufferedReader`:

```java
import java.io.*;

try {
    File file = new File("sample.txt"); // Create a File object for the file
to be read
    BufferedReader reader = new BufferedReader(new FileReader(file)); // Crea
te a BufferedReader
    String line;
    while ((line = reader.readLine()) != null) {
        System.out.println(line); // Read and print each line from the file
    }
    reader.close(); // Close the reader when done
} catch (IOException e) {
    e.printStackTrace();
}
```

In this example, we create a `File` object representing the file we want to read, wrap it in a `FileReader`, and then wrap the `FileReader` in a `BufferedReader` for efficient reading line by line.

Writing Files

To write data to a file, you can use classes like `File`, `FileOutputStream`, `BufferedWriter`, and `PrintWriter`. Here's a basic example using `PrintWriter`:

```java
import java.io.*;

try {
    File file = new File("output.txt"); // Create a File object for the file
to be written
    PrintWriter writer = new PrintWriter(new BufferedWriter(new FileWriter(fi
le))); // Create a PrintWriter
    writer.println("Hello, World!"); // Write a line to the file
    writer.close(); // Close the writer when done
} catch (IOException e) {
    e.printStackTrace();
}
```

In this example, we create a `File` object representing the file we want to write to, wrap it in a `FileWriter`, wrap the `FileWriter` in a `BufferedWriter` for efficiency, and finally wrap the `BufferedWriter` in a `PrintWriter` for easy writing of text.

Working with Directories

Java provides methods for working with directories, such as creating directories, listing files in a directory, and deleting directories. Here's an example of creating a directory and listing its contents:

```java
import java.io.*;

try {
    File directory = new File("my_directory"); // Create a directory
    if (directory.mkdir()) {
        System.out.println("Directory created successfully.");
    } else {
        System.out.println("Failed to create directory.");
    }

    File[] files = directory.listFiles(); // List files in the directory
    if (files != null) {
        System.out.println("Files in the directory:");
        for (File file : files) {
            System.out.println(file.getName());
        }
    }
} catch (Exception e) {
    e.printStackTrace();
}
```

Checking File and Directory Existence

You can check whether a file or directory exists using the `exists()` method:

```
File file = new File("sample.txt");
if (file.exists()) {
    System.out.println("File exists.");
} else {
    System.out.println("File does not exist.");
}
```

Deleting Files and Directories

To delete a file or directory, you can use the `delete()` method:

```
File file = new File("sample.txt");
if (file.delete()) {
    System.out.println("File deleted successfully.");
} else {
    System.out.println("Failed to delete file.");
}
```

For directories, you can use `delete()` to delete an empty directory or `deleteOnExit()` to schedule a directory to be deleted when the Java Virtual Machine (JVM) exits.

File I/O Exception Handling

When working with files and directories, it's crucial to handle exceptions properly. File I/O operations can throw various exceptions, such as `FileNotFoundException` and `IOException`. It's a good practice to use try-catch blocks to handle these exceptions gracefully.

File I/O operations are a fundamental part of many Java applications, enabling them to read and write data from and to external files and directories. Understanding how to perform file I/O operations effectively is essential for developing applications that work with data persistence and storage.

4.4 Date and Time Manipulation

Handling date and time is a common requirement in many Java applications, from simple date formatting to more complex operations like calculating intervals and working with time zones. The Java Standard Library provides classes and utilities in the `java.util` and `java.time` packages to handle date and time effectively.

Date and Time Basics

In Java, you can represent date and time using various classes, such as `java.util.Date`, `java.util.Calendar`, and the modern `java.time` classes introduced in Java 8. The `java.util.Date` class is a legacy class, and it's recommended to use the new `java.time` classes for better functionality and flexibility.

Here's an example of creating and displaying the current date and time using `java.util.Date`:

```java
import java.util.Date;

// Create a Date object representing the current date and time
Date currentDate = new Date();

// Display the current date and time
System.out.println("Current Date and Time: " + currentDate);
```

java.time Package

The `java.time` package introduced in Java 8 provides a modern and comprehensive API for working with date and time. Key classes in this package include `LocalDate`, `LocalTime`, `LocalDateTime`, `ZonedDateTime`, and more.

Here's an example of working with `LocalDate` to represent and manipulate dates:

```java
import java.time.LocalDate;

// Create a LocalDate object representing a specific date (e.g., November 15,
2023)
LocalDate date = LocalDate.of(2023, 11, 15);

// Perform date operations
LocalDate tomorrow = date.plusDays(1);
System.out.println("Tomorrow's Date: " + tomorrow);

// Check if a date is before or after another date
boolean isAfter = date.isAfter(LocalDate.now());
System.out.println("Is the date after today? " + isAfter);
```

Formatting Dates and Times

To format dates and times for display or storage, you can use the `DateTimeFormatter` class. It allows you to specify the desired format and convert date and time objects into strings:

```java
import java.time.LocalDateTime;
import java.time.format.DateTimeFormatter;

// Create a LocalDateTime object
LocalDateTime dateTime = LocalDateTime.now();

// Create a DateTimeFormatter for a custom format
DateTimeFormatter formatter = DateTimeFormatter.ofPattern("yyyy-MM-dd HH:mm:s
s");
```

```
// Format the date and time
String formattedDateTime = dateTime.format(formatter);
System.out.println("Formatted Date and Time: " + formattedDateTime);
```

Time Zones

Working with time zones is important when dealing with dates and times across different regions. The ZoneId class in the java.time package allows you to work with time zones effectively:

```
import java.time.ZoneId;
import java.time.ZonedDateTime;

// Create a ZonedDateTime object with a specific time zone (e.g., UTC)
ZoneId zoneId = ZoneId.of("UTC");
ZonedDateTime utcDateTime = ZonedDateTime.now(zoneId);

// Display the date and time in the specified time zone
System.out.println("UTC Date and Time: " + utcDateTime);
```

Calculating Date Intervals

You can calculate date intervals and perform date arithmetic using the java.time classes. For example, to calculate the number of days between two dates:

```
import java.time.LocalDate;
import java.time.Period;

LocalDate startDate = LocalDate.of(2023, 10, 1);
LocalDate endDate = LocalDate.of(2023, 10, 15);

// Calculate the period between two dates
Period period = Period.between(startDate, endDate);

// Get the number of days
int days = period.getDays();
System.out.println("Days between the two dates: " + days);
```

Date and Time API Best Practices

When working with dates and times, consider the following best practices:

1. Use the java.time classes: Whenever possible, use the modern java.time classes for date and time operations. They offer improved functionality and are more robust than the legacy java.util.Date and java.util.Calendar classes.

2. Handle time zones carefully: Be aware of time zones when working with date and time data, especially in applications that deal with international users or distributed systems.

3. Use DateTimeFormatter for formatting: When displaying or parsing dates and times, use DateTimeFormatter to ensure consistent formatting and parsing across different locales and regions.

4. Consider immutability: The java.time classes are immutable, meaning that they cannot be modified once created. This immutability is beneficial for thread safety and predictable behavior.

The ability to work with dates and times is crucial in many Java applications, from scheduling tasks to handling timestamps in databases. By using the java.time package and following best practices, you can perform date and time operations accurately and efficiently.

4.5 Collections Framework

The Java Collections Framework is a powerful set of classes and interfaces for working with collections of objects. Collections are used to store, retrieve, and manipulate groups of data, such as lists, sets, and maps. This framework provides a consistent and efficient way to manage data structures in Java applications.

Key Interfaces

The Java Collections Framework includes several key interfaces, each designed for specific use cases:

1. **Collection**: The root interface for all collection types. It represents a group of objects and defines basic methods like add, remove, size, and isEmpty.

2. **List**: An ordered collection that allows duplicate elements. Lists are typically implemented as arrays or linked lists. Common implementations include ArrayList and LinkedList.

3. **Set**: A collection that does not allow duplicate elements. Common implementations include HashSet and TreeSet.

4. **Map**: A collection that stores key-value pairs, where each key is associated with a value. Common implementations include HashMap and TreeMap.

Common Collection Implementations

List Implementations

- **ArrayList**: Implements a dynamic array that can grow as needed. It provides fast random access but may be slower when inserting or removing elements in the middle.

- **LinkedList**: Implements a doubly-linked list, which is efficient for insertions and removals in the middle but slower for random access.

- **HashSet**: Stores elements in a hash table, providing constant-time average performance for basic operations.

- **LinkedHashSet**: Maintains the order of elements, making it suitable when order matters and you need fast access.

- **TreeSet**: Stores elements in a sorted tree structure (e.g., red-black tree). Elements are ordered, making it useful for maintaining a sorted collection.

Map Implementations

- **HashMap**: Stores key-value pairs in a hash table, offering constant-time average performance for basic operations.

- **LinkedHashMap**: Maintains the order of key-value pairs, useful when you need to iterate through elements in a predictable order.

- **TreeMap**: Stores key-value pairs in a sorted tree structure, providing elements in sorted order.

Iterating Through Collections

To iterate through elements in a collection, you can use iterators or enhanced for loops (for-each loops). Here's an example using an enhanced for loop to iterate through a list:

```
List<String> names = new ArrayList<>();
names.add("Alice");
names.add("Bob");
names.add("Charlie");

for (String name : names) {
    System.out.println(name);
}
```

Sorting Collections

You can sort collections that implement the List interface using the Collections.sort() method or by using a TreeSet for sets. Here's an example of sorting a list of strings:

```
List<String> names = new ArrayList<>();
names.add("Charlie");
names.add("Alice");
names.add("Bob");

Collections.sort(names); // Sort the list

for (String name : names) {
    System.out.println(name);
}
```

Using Generics

The Java Collections Framework uses generics to ensure type safety. When declaring a collection, you can specify the type of elements it will contain. For example:

```
List<String> names = new ArrayList<>(); // List of strings
Set<Integer> numbers = new HashSet<>(); // Set of integers
Map<String, Integer> scores = new HashMap<>(); // Map of string keys and inte
ger values
```

Generics help prevent type errors at compile-time and provide better code readability.

Common Collection Operations

The Java Collections Framework provides a wide range of operations for manipulating collections, including adding and removing elements, checking for containment, finding elements, and more. These operations are common across different collection types, ensuring a consistent API for developers.

Here are some common collection operations:

- add(E element): Adds an element to the collection.
- remove(Object obj): Removes the specified element from the collection.
- contains(Object obj): Checks if the collection contains the specified element.
- size(): Returns the number of elements in the collection.
- isEmpty(): Checks if the collection is empty.
- clear(): Removes all elements from the collection.

Collections Utility Class

The java.util.Collections class provides various utility methods for working with collections, including sorting, shuffling, finding the minimum and maximum elements, and more. These methods are particularly helpful when dealing with collections.

In conclusion, the Java Collections Framework offers a rich set of classes and interfaces for working with collections of data. Whether you need to store a list of items, ensure uniqueness with a set, or map keys to values, the framework provides efficient and type-safe solutions for a wide range of use cases. Understanding these collections and their common operations is fundamental for Java developers working with data structures and algorithms.

Chapter 5: Advanced Java Features

5.1 Generics in Java

Generics in Java is a powerful feature that allows you to write classes, interfaces, and methods that operate on types as parameters. This enables you to create more flexible and type-safe code. Generics provide the ability to design classes and methods that work with different data types while maintaining type safety at compile time.

Introduction to Generics

In Java, generics are represented using angle brackets < > and involve type parameters. A generic class or method can work with different types by substituting the type parameters with actual types when the class is instantiated or the method is called.

Here's a simple example of a generic class called Box:

```java
public class Box<T> {
    private T content;

    public Box(T content) {
        this.content = content;
    }

    public T getContent() {
        return content;
    }
}
```

In this example, Box is a generic class with a type parameter T. It can be used to create boxes that can hold values of any type.

Using Generics for Type Safety

Generics provide type safety by allowing the compiler to catch type-related errors at compile time rather than at runtime. Consider the following example:

```java
Box<Integer> intBox = new Box<>(42);
Box<String> strBox = new Box<>("Hello");

int value1 = intBox.getContent(); // No casting needed
String value2 = strBox.getContent(); // No casting needed
```

With generics, the compiler ensures that you cannot accidentally mix types, and casting is unnecessary when retrieving values from a generic container.

Generic Methods

Generics can also be used with methods. You can create methods that accept or return generic types. Here's an example of a generic method to find the maximum of two values:

```java
public <T extends Comparable<T>> T findMax(T a, T b) {
    return a.compareTo(b) >= 0 ? a : b;
}
```

```java
// Usage
int maxInt = findMax(10, 20);
double maxDouble = findMax(3.14, 2.71);
```

In this example, the method findMax is generic and accepts parameters of any type that implements the Comparable interface. This allows you to find the maximum of different types in a type-safe manner.

Wildcards in Generics

Java generics also support wildcard types, denoted by the ? symbol. Wildcards are used when you want to work with an unknown type or when you want to specify bounds on a type parameter.

Here's an example of using a wildcard in a method to print elements from a list:

```java
public static void printList(List<?> list) {
    for (Object item : list) {
        System.out.println(item);
    }
}
```

The <?> wildcard allows you to pass a list of any type to the printList method.

Generic Classes and Subtyping

Generics in Java support subtyping. This means that if you have a generic class Box<T>, you can use a Box<U> where U is a subtype of T. For example:

```java
Box<Number> numberBox = new Box<>(42);
Box<Integer> intBox = new Box<>(10);

numberBox = intBox; // Allowed due to subtyping
```

Type Erasure

It's important to note that Java uses type erasure for generics. This means that generic type information is removed at runtime, and the compiled code uses the raw types. For example, List<String> and List<Integer> are both represented as List at runtime.

Benefits of Generics

Generics offer several advantages in Java programming:

- **Type Safety**: Generics help catch type-related errors at compile time, reducing the likelihood of runtime errors.

- **Code Reusability**: Generic classes and methods can be used with various data types, promoting code reuse.

- **Cleaner Code**: Generics eliminate the need for explicit type casting, resulting in cleaner and more readable code.

- **Flexibility**: Generics provide flexibility in designing classes and methods that work with different types.

In conclusion, generics in Java are a fundamental feature that enhances type safety and code reusability. They allow you to write more flexible and type-safe code by using type parameters in classes, interfaces, and methods. Understanding how to use generics is essential for developing robust and maintainable Java applications.

5.2 Lambda Expressions and Functional Interfaces

Lambda expressions, introduced in Java 8, are a significant feature that simplifies the creation of anonymous functions or "closures." They enable you to write more concise and readable code, especially when working with functional interfaces. This section explores lambda expressions, functional interfaces, and their usage in Java.

Lambda Expressions

A lambda expression is a concise way to represent an anonymous function that can have zero or more parameters and a body. Lambda expressions are particularly useful when you need to define a small piece of functionality to be passed as an argument to a method or used in a functional context.

Here's a simple example of a lambda expression that defines a function to calculate the square of a number:

```
// Lambda expression to calculate the square of a number
Function<Integer, Integer> square = x -> x * x;

// Using the lambda expression
int result = square.apply(5); // result will be 25
```

In this example, Function<Integer, Integer> represents a functional interface with a single abstract method (apply) that takes an Integer as input and returns an Integer. The lambda expression x -> x * x defines the implementation of the apply method.

Functional Interfaces

A functional interface is an interface with exactly one abstract method, often referred to as the "single abstract method" or SAM. Functional interfaces play a crucial role in lambda expressions because they provide the target type for lambda expressions.

Java provides several built-in functional interfaces in the `java.util.function` package, such as `Function`, `Predicate`, and `Consumer`. These functional interfaces cover common use cases for lambda expressions.

Here's an example of using a functional interface and a lambda expression to filter a list of integers:

```
List<Integer> numbers = Arrays.asList(1, 2, 3, 4, 5, 6, 7, 8, 9);

// Using a lambda expression to filter even numbers
List<Integer> evenNumbers = numbers.stream()
    .filter(x -> x % 2 == 0)
    .collect(Collectors.toList());
```

In this example, `filter` takes a `Predicate` (a functional interface that represents a condition) as an argument. The lambda expression `x -> x % 2 == 0` serves as the implementation of the `test` method in the `Predicate` interface.

Method References

Method references are another feature introduced in Java 8 that simplify lambda expressions further when calling an existing method. Method references allow you to reference methods directly by their names instead of providing a lambda expression. They are especially useful when a lambda expression simply calls an existing method.

Here's an example of using a method reference to sort a list of strings:

```
List<String> names = Arrays.asList("Alice", "Bob", "Charlie", "David");

// Using a method reference to sort strings
names.sort(String::compareToIgnoreCase);
```

In this example, `String::compareToIgnoreCase` is a method reference that refers to the `compareToIgnoreCase` method of the `String` class. It simplifies the sorting process by using an existing method.

Capturing Variables

Lambda expressions can capture variables from their surrounding scope. These captured variables are effectively final or "effectively" final, meaning they are not allowed to be modified inside the lambda expression. This is known as "variable capture."

Here's an example of capturing a variable in a lambda expression:

```
int multiplier = 2;

// Lambda expression that captures the multiplier variable
Function<Integer, Integer> multiplyByMultiplier = x -> x * multiplier;

int result = multiplyByMultiplier.apply(5); // result will be 10
```

In this example, the lambda expression x -> x * multiplier captures the multiplier variable from the surrounding scope.

Lambda Expression Syntax

Lambda expressions have a simple syntax:

- `(parameter1, parameter2, ...) -> { body }`

The parameters are enclosed in parentheses, followed by the -> symbol, and the body is enclosed in braces (if it contains more than one statement) or can be a single expression without braces.

Benefits of Lambda Expressions

Lambda expressions offer several benefits in Java:

- **Conciseness**: Lambda expressions make code more concise and readable, especially for small functions.

- **Functional Programming**: They enable functional programming style, allowing you to treat functions as first-class citizens.

- **Improved APIs**: Java's standard libraries use lambda expressions to improve APIs, making them more flexible and expressive.

- **Parallel Processing**: Lambda expressions can be used effectively with parallel streams for concurrent and parallel processing.

In conclusion, lambda expressions and functional interfaces introduced in Java 8 have revolutionized Java programming by simplifying the creation of anonymous functions and promoting functional programming practices. They provide a concise and expressive way to work with functions and are widely used in modern Java development.

5.3 Streams and Stream API

The Stream API, introduced in Java 8, is a powerful tool for processing sequences of data elements. Streams enable you to express complex data processing operations in a more concise and functional style, making your code easier to read and maintain. This section explores the Stream API and how it simplifies data manipulation in Java.

What is a Stream?

A stream is a sequence of elements that can be processed sequentially or in parallel. Elements in a stream can be any data type, including objects, numbers, or other data structures. You can create streams from various sources, such as collections, arrays, or even by generating elements on the fly.

Here's an example of creating a stream from a list of numbers:

```
List<Integer> numbers = Arrays.asList(1, 2, 3, 4, 5);

// Create a stream from the list
Stream<Integer> numberStream = numbers.stream();
```

Stream Operations

Streams support a wide range of operations, which can be divided into two categories: intermediate and terminal operations.

Intermediate Operations

Intermediate operations are operations that transform a stream into another stream. These operations are often chained together to create a pipeline of transformations. Some common intermediate operations include:

- `filter(Predicate<T> predicate)`: Filters the stream based on a condition defined by the predicate function.
- `map(Function<T, R> mapper)`: Applies the mapper function to each element and transforms the stream into a stream of a different type.
- `sorted()`: Sorts the elements in the stream.
- `distinct()`: Removes duplicate elements from the stream.

Here's an example of using intermediate operations to filter and map a stream of numbers:

```
List<Integer> numbers = Arrays.asList(1, 2, 3, 4, 5);

// Create a stream from the list and perform intermediate operations
List<Integer> result = numbers.stream()
    .filter(n -> n % 2 == 0) // Keep only even numbers
    .map(n -> n * 2) // Double each number
    .collect(Collectors.toList()); // Collect the result into a list

// Result: [4, 8]
```

Terminal Operations

Terminal operations are operations that produce a result or a side-effect. They terminate the stream and cannot be chained together. Some common terminal operations include:

- `forEach(Consumer<T> action)`: Performs an action on each element of the stream.

- collect(Collector<T, A, R> collector): Collects the elements of the stream into a collection or another data structure.
- reduce(T identity, BinaryOperator<T> accumulator): Performs a reduction operation on the elements of the stream.
- count(): Returns the count of elements in the stream.
- anyMatch(Predicate<T> predicate): Checks if any element in the stream matches a given condition.

Here's an example of using terminal operations to print elements and find the sum of a stream of numbers:

```
List<Integer> numbers = Arrays.asList(1, 2, 3, 4, 5);

// Create a stream from the list and perform terminal operations
numbers.stream()
    .forEach(System.out::println); // Print each element

int sum = numbers.stream()
    .reduce(0, (a, b) -> a + b); // Calculate the sum

// Sum: 15
```

Lazy Evaluation

One of the key features of streams is lazy evaluation. Intermediate operations do not process elements until a terminal operation is invoked. This allows for more efficient processing, especially when working with large data sets.

```
List<Integer> numbers = Arrays.asList(1, 2, 3, 4, 5);

// This intermediate operation doesn't execute until a terminal operation is
invoked
Stream<Integer> doubledNumbers = numbers.stream()
    .map(n -> {
        System.out.println("Doubling " + n);
        return n * 2;
    });

// No output yet

doubledNumbers.forEach(System.out::println); // Terminal operation

// Output:
// Doubling 1
// Doubling 2
// Doubling 3
// Doubling 4
// Doubling 5
// 2
```

```
// 4
// 6
// 8
// 10
```

Parallel Streams

Streams can be processed in parallel using the `parallelStream()` method instead of `stream()`. This can significantly improve performance for operations that can be parallelized, such as filtering and mapping.

```java
List<Integer> numbers = Arrays.asList(1, 2, 3, 4, 5);

// Create a parallel stream and perform operations in parallel
int sum = numbers.parallelStream()
    .filter(n -> n % 2 == 0) // Keep only even numbers
    .mapToInt(Integer::intValue) // Convert to primitive int
    .sum(); // Calculate the sum in parallel

// Sum: 6
```

Benefits of Streams

Streams offer several advantages in Java programming:

- **Conciseness**: Streams allow you to express complex data processing operations in a concise and readable manner.

- **Readability**: Streams encourage a functional programming style, which often results in more readable and maintainable code.

- **Parallel Processing**: Streams can easily be parallelized, allowing for improved performance on multi-core processors.

- **Lazy Evaluation**: Lazy evaluation reduces unnecessary computation and improves efficiency.

In conclusion, the Stream API in Java provides a powerful and expressive way to work with sequences of data elements. Whether you're filtering, mapping, or reducing data, streams simplify complex operations and promote a functional programming style. Understanding how to use streams is essential for modern Java developers seeking to write more efficient and readable code.

5.4 Concurrency and Multithreading

Concurrency and multithreading are essential concepts in modern software development, allowing applications to perform multiple tasks simultaneously and efficiently utilize multi-core processors. In Java, concurrency is achieved through the use of threads and the Java

Concurrency API. This section explores the fundamentals of concurrency and multithreading in Java.

What is Concurrency?

Concurrency is the concept of multiple tasks making progress in overlapping time periods. It doesn't necessarily mean that tasks are executing simultaneously, as they might be interleaved in execution. Concurrency is especially important in applications that need to perform tasks concurrently for responsiveness and performance reasons.

In Java, threads are the primary unit of concurrent execution. A thread is a lightweight, independent process within a Java application that can execute code concurrently with other threads.

Creating Threads

In Java, you can create threads in two ways: by extending the Thread class or by implementing the Runnable interface. The latter is the recommended approach, as it allows better separation of the thread's behavior from the class's inheritance hierarchy.

Here's an example of creating a thread by implementing Runnable:

```java
public class MyRunnable implements Runnable {
    @Override
    public void run() {
        // Code to be executed by the thread
        System.out.println("Thread is running.");
    }
}

public class Main {
    public static void main(String[] args) {
        // Create a thread and pass the runnable object to it
        Thread myThread = new Thread(new MyRunnable());

        // Start the thread
        myThread.start();
    }
}
```

Thread States

Threads in Java can be in various states during their lifecycle, including:

- **New**: The thread has been created but has not started yet.
- **Runnable**: The thread is executing, or it is ready to run.
- **Blocked**: The thread is waiting for a resource, such as I/O or synchronization locks.
- **Waiting**: The thread is waiting for another thread to perform a specific action.
- **Timed Waiting**: The thread is waiting for a specified time.

- **Terminated**: The thread has completed its execution.

Thread Synchronization

Concurrency introduces challenges related to data access and synchronization. When multiple threads access shared resources concurrently, it can lead to data inconsistencies or race conditions. Java provides mechanisms for thread synchronization, including the synchronized keyword and the java.util.concurrent package.

Here's an example of using synchronized to protect a shared resource:

```java
public class Counter {
    private int count = 0;

    public synchronized void increment() {
        count++;
    }

    public synchronized int getCount() {
        return count;
    }
}
```

In this example, the increment and getCount methods are synchronized, ensuring that only one thread can execute them at a time, preventing data corruption.

Java Concurrency API

Java provides a rich set of classes and interfaces in the java.util.concurrent package to simplify multithreaded programming. Some important classes and interfaces in the Java Concurrency API include:

- Executor: An interface for executing tasks asynchronously.
- ExecutorService: A higher-level interface for managing and controlling thread execution.
- ThreadPoolExecutor: A versatile implementation of the ExecutorService interface.
- Future: An interface representing the result of an asynchronous computation.
- BlockingQueue: An interface for managing data transfer between threads.
- Semaphore and CountDownLatch: Classes for controlling access to resources and synchronization.

Thread Pools

Thread pools are a common way to manage threads efficiently. Instead of creating a new thread for each task, a thread pool maintains a pool of threads and reuses them for executing tasks. This reduces the overhead of creating and destroying threads and provides better control over thread execution.

Here's an example of creating a thread pool:

```
ExecutorService executorService = Executors.newFixedThreadPool(4);

// Submit tasks to the thread pool
executorService.submit(task1);
executorService.submit(task2);
executorService.submit(task3);

// Shutdown the thread pool when done
executorService.shutdown();
```

Java Memory Model (JMM)

The Java Memory Model defines the rules and guarantees regarding the visibility and ordering of memory operations in a multithreaded environment. Understanding the JMM is crucial for writing correct and thread-safe concurrent programs in Java.

Benefits of Concurrency

Concurrency and multithreading offer several advantages in Java programming:

- **Improved Performance**: Multithreading can utilize multiple CPU cores, leading to improved performance for CPU-bound tasks.

- **Responsiveness**: Concurrency allows applications to remain responsive by handling tasks concurrently, such as responding to user input while performing background tasks.

- **Resource Utilization**: Concurrency enables better utilization of system resources, making efficient use of CPU time.

- **Parallelism**: Multithreading supports parallelism, which is essential for high-performance computing and data processing.

In conclusion, concurrency and multithreading are fundamental concepts in Java programming that enable applications to perform tasks concurrently, leading to improved performance, responsiveness, and resource utilization. Understanding how to create, synchronize, and manage threads is essential for writing efficient and reliable concurrent Java applications.

5.5 Reflection and Annotations

Reflection and annotations are advanced features in Java that provide the ability to inspect and manipulate classes, methods, fields, and other program elements at runtime. These features are often used in frameworks, libraries, and tools to achieve various tasks, such as dependency injection, serialization, and dynamic code generation. This section explores reflection and annotations in Java.

Reflection

Reflection is the process of examining and manipulating the structure, behavior, and metadata of classes, methods, fields, and other program elements at runtime. Java provides the `java.lang.reflect` package for reflection-related operations.

Accessing Class Information

You can use reflection to access class information, including methods, fields, constructors, and annotations. Here's an example of how to get class information using reflection:

```
Class<?> clazz = MyClass.class;

// Get class name
String className = clazz.getName();

// Get class modifiers
int modifiers = clazz.getModifiers();

// Get superclasses
Class<?> superClass = clazz.getSuperclass();

// Get interfaces implemented by the class
Class<?>[] interfaces = clazz.getInterfaces();
```

Accessing Method Information

Reflection allows you to inspect and invoke methods dynamically. You can obtain method information, such as name, parameters, return type, and modifiers, using reflection:

```
Method method = clazz.getMethod("methodName", parameterTypes);

String methodName = method.getName();
Class<?> returnType = method.getReturnType();
int modifiers = method.getModifiers();
```

You can also invoke methods dynamically, even if you don't know the method at compile time:

```
Object instance = clazz.newInstance();
Object result = method.invoke(instance, args);
```

Accessing Field Information

Reflection enables you to access fields of a class, including their name, type, and modifiers:

```
Field field = clazz.getDeclaredField("fieldName");

String fieldName = field.getName();
Class<?> fieldType = field.getType();
int modifiers = field.getModifiers();
```

You can also set and get field values dynamically:

```
Object instance = clazz.newInstance();
field.setAccessible(true); // For private fields
Object value = field.get(instance);
field.set(instance, newValue);
```

Working with Annotations

Reflection allows you to work with annotations, which provide metadata about classes, methods, fields, and other program elements. You can inspect and access annotations using reflection:

```
Annotation annotation = method.getAnnotation(MyAnnotation.class);

if (annotation != null) {
    // Process annotation
    String value = ((MyAnnotation) annotation).value();
}
```

Reflection is a powerful feature, but it should be used judiciously, as it can lead to decreased performance and type safety. It's often used in frameworks like Spring and Hibernate to provide flexible and extensible behavior.

Annotations

Annotations are metadata that can be added to classes, methods, fields, and other program elements to provide additional information or instructions to the compiler or runtime environment. Java annotations are defined using the @ symbol, followed by the annotation name.

Built-In Annotations

Java provides several built-in annotations, such as @Override, @Deprecated, and @SuppressWarnings, which have specific meanings and are used by the compiler and tools.

For example, the @Override annotation is used to indicate that a method in a subclass is intended to override a method in its superclass:

```
@Override
public void someMethod() {
    // Override superclass method
}
```

Custom Annotations

You can also create custom annotations by defining your own annotation types. Custom annotations are often used to add metadata or configuration to classes, methods, or fields in your application.

Here's an example of defining a custom annotation:

```java
import java.lang.annotation.*;

@Retention(RetentionPolicy.RUNTIME)
@Target(ElementType.METHOD)
public @interface MyAnnotation {
    String value() default "default value";
}
```

In this example, `@MyAnnotation` is a custom annotation with a single `value` element.

Using Custom Annotations

You can use custom annotations to annotate program elements and access them using reflection. Here's how you can use the `@MyAnnotation` annotation:

```java
@MyAnnotation("custom value")
public void myMethod() {
    // Method implementation
}
```

You can access the annotation and its values using reflection, as shown earlier.

Annotations are extensively used in various Java frameworks and libraries for tasks such as dependency injection, configuration, and persistence mapping. They provide a flexible and extensible way to add metadata and behavior to your code.

In conclusion, reflection and annotations are powerful features in Java that allow you to inspect and manipulate classes, methods, fields, and annotations at runtime. While they provide great flexibility and extensibility, they should be used carefully, as they can lead to decreased performance and reduced type safety. Understanding how to use reflection and create custom annotations is essential for advanced Java development and working with various frameworks and libraries.

Chapter 6: Graphical User Interfaces with JavaFX

6.1 Introduction to JavaFX

JavaFX is a modern, rich client platform for building cross-platform applications with visually appealing user interfaces. It provides a set of libraries and tools for creating interactive and visually stunning applications, including desktop applications, mobile apps, and embedded systems. In this section, we'll introduce you to the basics of JavaFX and its key features.

Key Features of JavaFX

JavaFX offers several features that make it a powerful choice for building graphical user interfaces (GUIs):

1. **Rich UI Controls:** JavaFX provides a wide range of built-in UI controls like buttons, text fields, tables, and charts. These controls are highly customizable, allowing you to create sophisticated user interfaces.

2. **Scene Graph:** JavaFX uses a hierarchical scene graph to represent the visual elements of your application. This makes it easy to organize and manipulate UI components.

3. **Styling and Theming:** JavaFX supports CSS for styling your application's UI. You can create visually appealing designs by applying styles and themes.

4. **2D and 3D Graphics:** JavaFX includes support for both 2D and 3D graphics, making it suitable for games, simulations, and data visualization.

5. **Animation:** JavaFX provides a robust animation framework for creating smooth and interactive animations, transitions, and effects.

6. **Media Support:** You can integrate audio and video playback seamlessly into your JavaFX applications.

7. **FXML and Scene Builder:** FXML is an XML-based markup language for designing UIs in JavaFX. Scene Builder is a visual layout tool that simplifies UI design.

8. **Event Handling:** JavaFX allows you to handle user interactions and events efficiently, providing a responsive user experience.

Setting Up JavaFX

To start using JavaFX, you need to set up your development environment. JavaFX is included with Java SE 8 and later versions. Here are the basic steps to get started:

1. **Install Java:** Ensure you have Java Development Kit (JDK) 8 or later installed on your system.

2. **Create a JavaFX Project:** You can create a JavaFX project using popular Java IDEs like IntelliJ IDEA, Eclipse, or NetBeans. These IDEs often provide templates for JavaFX projects.

3. **Add JavaFX Libraries:** Make sure your project is configured to include the JavaFX libraries. You may need to specify the JavaFX SDK path in your project settings.

Hello World in JavaFX

Let's create a simple JavaFX "Hello World" application to get a feel for how JavaFX works. Here's a basic example:

```java
import javafx.application.Application;
import javafx.scene.Scene;
import javafx.scene.control.Label;
import javafx.stage.Stage;

public class HelloWorldApp extends Application {
    @Override
    public void start(Stage primaryStage) {
        Label label = new Label("Hello, JavaFX!");
        Scene scene = new Scene(label, 300, 200);

        primaryStage.setTitle("Hello JavaFX Example");
        primaryStage.setScene(scene);
        primaryStage.show();
    }

    public static void main(String[] args) {
        launch(args);
    }
}
```

In this example, we create a simple JavaFX application with a window that displays the text "Hello, JavaFX!". The start method sets up the UI, and the main method is the entry point for our application.

This is just a basic introduction to JavaFX. In the following sections, we will explore various aspects of JavaFX in more detail, including building complex user interfaces, handling events, and creating interactive applications.

6.2 Building User Interfaces with JavaFX

JavaFX provides a rich set of UI controls and layout containers for building user interfaces (UIs) for your applications. In this section, we'll explore how to create UIs in JavaFX, including adding controls, arranging them in layouts, and applying styles.

UI Controls in JavaFX

JavaFX offers a wide range of UI controls that you can use to create interactive applications. Some common UI controls include:

- **Button:** Used for triggering actions when clicked.
- **Label:** Displays static text or information.
- **TextField:** Allows users to input text.
- **TextArea:** Provides a multiline text input field.
- **ComboBox:** A dropdown list of items for selection.
- **RadioButton and CheckBox:** Used for single and multiple selections, respectively.
- **ListView and TableView:** Display lists or tables of data.
- **Slider and ProgressBar:** Visualize and control values within a range.
- **FileChooser and DirectoryChooser:** Enable file and directory selection.

You can add these controls to your JavaFX application's scene graph to build the user interface.

Layout Managers

JavaFX provides various layout containers to help you arrange and organize UI controls efficiently. Some commonly used layout containers include:

- **VBox and HBox:** Vertical and horizontal boxes for stacking controls.
- **GridPane:** A grid-based layout manager.
- **BorderPane:** Divides the layout into top, bottom, left, right, and center regions.
- **StackPane:** Stacks controls on top of each other.
- **AnchorPane:** Allows precise control of child node placement using absolute coordinates.

Layout managers help you create responsive and well-structured UIs that adapt to different screen sizes and orientations.

Styling with CSS

JavaFX allows you to style your UI using Cascading Style Sheets (CSS). You can apply styles to individual controls or entire scenes to achieve a consistent and visually appealing design. Here's an example of how to apply CSS styles to a JavaFX button:

```java
import javafx.application.Application;
import javafx.scene.Scene;
import javafx.scene.control.Button;
import javafx.scene.layout.VBox;
import javafx.stage.Stage;

public class StyledButtonApp extends Application {
    @Override
    public void start(Stage primaryStage) {
```

```
        Button button = new Button("Styled Button");
        button.setStyle("-fx-background-color: #3498db; -fx-text-fill: white;
-fx-font-size: 14px;");

        VBox root = new VBox(button);
        Scene scene = new Scene(root, 300, 200);

        primaryStage.setTitle("Styled Button Example");
        primaryStage.setScene(scene);
        primaryStage.show();
    }

    public static void main(String[] args) {
        launch(args);
    }
}
```

In this example, we create a styled button with a blue background and white text. You can define more complex styles using CSS properties to achieve the desired look and feel for your application.

Event Handling

JavaFX provides robust event handling mechanisms to respond to user interactions and actions on UI controls. You can attach event handlers to controls to perform actions when events occur. Common events include button clicks, mouse events, keyboard input, and more.

Here's a simple example of attaching a click event handler to a button:

```
button.setOnAction(e -> {
    // Code to execute when the button is clicked
    System.out.println("Button clicked!");
});
```

This code prints "Button clicked!" to the console when the button is clicked.

These are the fundamental aspects of building user interfaces in JavaFX. As you become more familiar with JavaFX, you can create more complex and interactive UIs for your applications.

6.3 Event Handling in JavaFX

Event handling is a crucial aspect of creating interactive applications with JavaFX. Events are generated in response to user actions or other activities within the application. In this section, we'll explore how event handling works in JavaFX and how you can respond to various types of events.

JavaFX supports a wide range of event types, including:

- **ActionEvent:** Triggered by user actions like button clicks.
- **MouseEvent:** Generated when the mouse interacts with UI elements, including clicks, moves, and scrolls.
- **KeyEvent:** Captures keyboard input, including key presses and releases.
- **DragEvent and DropEvent:** Handle drag-and-drop operations.
- **TouchEvent:** Designed for touch-based interfaces, capturing touch events.
- **WindowEvent:** Deals with window-related events, such as resizing and closing.
- **Event:** The base class for all events in JavaFX.

Event Handling Mechanisms

There are two primary mechanisms for handling events in JavaFX:

1. **Declarative Event Handling:** In this approach, you define event handlers directly within your FXML or code. For example, you can attach an onAction handler to a button in FXML or set an event handler in Java code.

```
<Button text="Click Me" onAction="#handleButtonClick" />

button.setOnAction(e -> {
    // Event handling logic here
});
```

2. **Event Filters and Handlers:** JavaFX allows you to use event filters and event handlers to capture and respond to events. Event filters are executed before the event reaches the target node, while event handlers are executed after the event reaches the target node.

```
// Event filter example
button.addEventFilter(MouseEvent.MOUSE_CLICKED, e -> {
    // Event filter logic here
});

// Event handler example
button.setOnMouseClicked(e -> {
    // Event handler logic here
});
```

Event Propagation

Events in JavaFX follow a bubbling and capturing mechanism. When an event occurs, it can propagate through the scene graph in two directions:

- **Bubbling:** Events start from the target node and move up the hierarchy of parent nodes. This allows you to handle events at different levels of the scene graph.

- **Capturing:** Events start from the root of the scene graph and move towards the target node. This can be useful for global event handling or intercepting events before they reach the target.

Let's consider an example of handling a button click event:

```java
button.setOnAction(e -> {
    // Event handling logic here
    System.out.println("Button clicked!");
});
```

In this code, we attach an event handler to a button. When the button is clicked, the code inside the handler is executed, and "Button clicked!" is printed to the console.

You can also access event information within the handler. For example, to get the source of the event:

```java
button.setOnAction(e -> {
    // Get the source of the event
    Button sourceButton = (Button) e.getSource();
    System.out.println("Button clicked: " + sourceButton.getText());
});
```

This code retrieves the source of the event (the button) and prints its text.

Conclusion

Event handling is a fundamental aspect of creating interactive JavaFX applications. Understanding event types, mechanisms, and propagation allows you to build responsive and user-friendly interfaces that respond to user interactions and actions. Whether you're building simple button clicks or complex drag-and-drop functionality, JavaFX provides the tools you need for effective event handling.

6.4 Layout Management in JavaFX

Layout management plays a crucial role in creating well-structured and responsive user interfaces in JavaFX applications. In this section, we'll delve into the concept of layout management and explore various layout containers and techniques provided by JavaFX.

The Importance of Layout Management

Layout management is essential because it determines how UI components are arranged and resized within a container. It ensures that your application's user interface adapts to different screen sizes, orientations, and resolutions, providing a consistent and user-friendly experience.

JavaFX provides a variety of layout containers that you can use to organize and position UI elements. Some of the most commonly used layout containers include:

1. **VBox (Vertical Box):** It arranges child nodes in a single vertical column, stacking them one below the other. This is useful for creating simple vertical layouts.

2. **HBox (Horizontal Box):** It arranges child nodes in a single horizontal row, placing them side by side. HBox is suitable for horizontal layouts.

3. **BorderPane:** This container divides the layout into five regions: top, bottom, left, right, and center. It's useful for creating layouts with a central content area surrounded by other UI elements like menus or toolbars.

4. **GridPane:** GridPane allows you to arrange nodes in rows and columns, making it suitable for complex grid-based layouts. You can specify the placement of nodes in specific grid cells.

5. **StackPane:** StackPane stacks child nodes on top of each other, allowing you to layer multiple UI elements. It's often used for layering graphics or creating overlays.

6. **AnchorPane:** AnchorPane allows precise positioning of child nodes using absolute coordinates or relative to the edges of the parent container. It's useful for creating pixel-perfect layouts.

Example: Using VBox and HBox

Let's look at a simple example of using VBox and HBox to create a basic layout:

```java
import javafx.application.Application;
import javafx.scene.Scene;
import javafx.scene.control.Button;
import javafx.scene.layout.HBox;
import javafx.scene.layout.VBox;
import javafx.stage.Stage;

public class LayoutExample extends Application {
    @Override
    public void start(Stage primaryStage) {
        VBox vBox = new VBox();  // Vertical layout container
        HBox hBox = new HBox();  // Horizontal layout container

        Button button1 = new Button("Button 1");
        Button button2 = new Button("Button 2");
        Button button3 = new Button("Button 3");

        // Add buttons to the horizontal layout
        hBox.getChildren().addAll(button1, button2, button3);
```

```
    Button button4 = new Button("Button 4");

    // Add horizontal Layout and another button to the vertical Layout
    vBox.getChildren().addAll(hBox, button4);

    Scene scene = new Scene(vBox, 300, 200);

    primaryStage.setTitle("Layout Example");
    primaryStage.setScene(scene);
    primaryStage.show();
    }

    public static void main(String[] args) {
        launch(args);
    }
}
```

In this example, we create a VBox and an HBox to arrange buttons both vertically and horizontally. This demonstrates the flexibility of layout containers in JavaFX.

Responsive Design

Responsive design is an essential aspect of layout management. JavaFX provides features like setting constraints, minimum and maximum sizes, and alignment options to ensure your UI adapts to different screen sizes and orientations.

Layout management is a fundamental skill in JavaFX development, and mastering it allows you to create visually appealing and user-friendly applications that work seamlessly across various devices and screen sizes.

6.5 Advanced JavaFX Features

JavaFX offers a wide range of advanced features that enable you to create sophisticated and interactive user interfaces. In this section, we'll explore some of these advanced features and how they can enhance your JavaFX applications.

1. Custom Controls

JavaFX allows you to create custom UI controls tailored to your application's specific needs. You can extend existing controls or build entirely new ones by combining existing JavaFX nodes. This enables you to create unique user interface elements that seamlessly integrate with the JavaFX framework.

Creating a custom control involves defining the control's appearance, behavior, and properties. You can use techniques like CSS styling and event handling to make your custom control look and behave just the way you want.

2. Animation and Transitions

JavaFX provides powerful animation and transition capabilities that allow you to add dynamic and visually appealing effects to your user interfaces. You can create animations for UI elements like transitions, fades, rotations, and scaling.

For example, you can animate the movement of a node across the screen, create smooth transitions between scenes, or add visual effects to user interactions. Animation in JavaFX is timeline-based and can be defined using the `Timeline` class.

3. 3D Graphics

While JavaFX is primarily a 2D graphics library, it also offers support for 3D graphics through the `javafx.scene.shape` package. You can create 3D scenes, add 3D shapes, and apply materials to them to achieve 3D effects in your applications.

JavaFX's 3D capabilities allow you to build interactive 3D visualizations, games, and simulations. You can control the camera perspective, lighting, and shading to create realistic 3D environments.

4. WebView Integration

JavaFX includes a WebView component that allows you to embed web content, such as HTML, CSS, and JavaScript, within your JavaFX applications. This integration enables you to display web-based content alongside your native JavaFX user interface.

WebView is particularly useful when you need to display web pages, render rich text, or interact with web-based APIs within your JavaFX application. You can also communicate between JavaFX and JavaScript code running in the WebView.

5. Accessibility Features

JavaFX places a strong emphasis on accessibility, making it possible to create applications that are usable by individuals with disabilities. It provides built-in support for screen readers and includes features like accessible names, descriptions, and roles for UI elements.

By following best practices for accessibility in JavaFX, you can ensure that your applications are inclusive and comply with accessibility standards, making them accessible to a wider audience.

6. Interoperability with Swing and AWT

JavaFX can be integrated with Swing and AWT (Abstract Window Toolkit) components, allowing you to leverage existing Swing or AWT libraries within your JavaFX applications. This is particularly useful when migrating legacy applications to JavaFX or when you need to use specific third-party Swing or AWT components.

You can embed Swing or AWT components within a JavaFX application using the `SwingNode` and `AWTFrame` classes, respectively.

These advanced features expand the capabilities of JavaFX, making it a versatile platform for building a wide range of applications, from modern and responsive user interfaces to games and data visualizations. By mastering these features, you can take your JavaFX development skills to the next level and create compelling user experiences.

Chapter 7: Database Programming with JDBC

7.1 Connecting to Databases

Java Database Connectivity (JDBC) is a Java-based framework that allows Java applications to interact with relational databases. In this section, we'll explore the fundamentals of connecting to databases using JDBC and how to perform basic database operations.

JDBC Overview

JDBC provides a standardized API for connecting to databases, executing SQL queries, and processing query results. It enables Java applications to communicate with various database systems such as MySQL, Oracle, PostgreSQL, and SQL Server.

To use JDBC, you need a JDBC driver specific to your database system. These drivers act as a bridge between your Java application and the database server. You typically include the JDBC driver library in your project to establish a connection.

Establishing a Database Connection

To connect to a database using JDBC, you follow these steps:

1. **Load the JDBC Driver:** Before you can establish a connection, load the JDBC driver for your database system. This is typically done using the `Class.forName()` method.

   ```java
   // Load the MySQL JDBC driver
   Class.forName("com.mysql.cj.jdbc.Driver");
   ```

2. **Create a Connection:** Use the `DriverManager.getConnection()` method to create a connection to the database. You need to provide the database URL, username, and password.

   ```java
   String url = "jdbc:mysql://localhost:3306/mydb";
   String username = "user";
   String password = "password";
   Connection connection = DriverManager.getConnection(url, username, password);
   ```

   Here, `url` is the JDBC URL for the database, which includes the hostname, port, and database name.

3. **Close the Connection:** After you're done with the database connection, it's essential to close it to release resources.

   ```java
   connection.close();
   ```

Handling Exceptions

When working with databases, it's crucial to handle exceptions properly. JDBC methods can throw exceptions related to database access, SQL syntax errors, or connection issues. You should use try-catch blocks to handle these exceptions gracefully.

```java
try {
    // JDBC code that may throw exceptions
} catch (SQLException e) {
    // Handle database-related exceptions
    e.printStackTrace();
} catch (Exception e) {
    // Handle other exceptions
    e.printStackTrace();
} finally {
    // Close resources in the finally block
    try {
        if (connection != null) {
            connection.close();
        }
    } catch (SQLException e) {
        e.printStackTrace();
    }
}
```

Using Connection Pools

In real-world applications, it's common to use connection pooling libraries like Apache DBCP or HikariCP to manage database connections efficiently. Connection pooling reduces the overhead of creating and closing connections for each database operation.

Connection pools maintain a pool of reusable connections that can be acquired and returned as needed, improving the performance and scalability of database operations.

Conclusion

Connecting to databases using JDBC is a fundamental skill for Java developers working with relational databases. JDBC provides a straightforward way to establish connections, execute SQL queries, and manage database interactions within your Java applications. By following best practices and handling exceptions properly, you can ensure robust and reliable database connectivity in your projects.

7.2 Executing SQL Queries in Java

Once you've established a database connection using JDBC, the next step is to execute SQL queries and retrieve data from the database. In this section, we'll explore how to execute SQL queries in Java using JDBC.

Creating Statements

To execute SQL queries, you need to create a `Statement` or a `PreparedStatement` object. These objects allow you to send SQL commands to the database.

1. **Statement:** The `Statement` interface is used for executing simple SQL queries without parameters. It's suitable for queries that don't involve user input.

   ```
   Statement statement = connection.createStatement();
   ```

2. **PreparedStatement:** The `PreparedStatement` interface is used for executing SQL queries with parameters. It's more secure and efficient when dealing with user input because it prevents SQL injection attacks.

   ```
   String sql = "SELECT * FROM users WHERE username = ?";
   PreparedStatement preparedStatement = connection.prepareStatement(sql);
   ```

Executing Queries

To execute SQL queries, you can use the `executeQuery()` method of the `Statement` or `PreparedStatement` objects. This method returns a `ResultSet` that contains the query results.

```
String sql = "SELECT * FROM employees";
ResultSet resultSet = statement.executeQuery(sql);

// Process the ResultSet
while (resultSet.next()) {
    int employeeId = resultSet.getInt("employee_id");
    String firstName = resultSet.getString("first_name");
    String lastName = resultSet.getString("last_name");
    // Process the retrieved data
}
```

Executing Updates

In addition to querying data, you can also execute SQL statements that modify the database, such as INSERT, UPDATE, or DELETE statements. For these operations, you can use the `executeUpdate()` method of the `Statement` or `PreparedStatement` objects.

```
String insertSql = "INSERT INTO students (name, age) VALUES (?, ?)";
PreparedStatement insertStatement = connection.prepareStatement(insertSql);
insertStatement.setString(1, "John Doe");
insertStatement.setInt(2, 25);
int rowsInserted = insertStatement.executeUpdate();

String updateSql = "UPDATE employees SET salary = ? WHERE department = ?";
PreparedStatement updateStatement = connection.prepareStatement(updateSql);
updateStatement.setDouble(1, 50000.0);
updateStatement.setString(2, "HR");
int rowsUpdated = updateStatement.executeUpdate();
```

Closing Resources

After executing SQL queries or updates, it's crucial to close the `ResultSet`, `Statement`, and `Connection` objects to release resources and avoid memory leaks.

```
resultSet.close();
statement.close();
connection.close();
```

Handling Exceptions

When working with SQL queries and updates, you should handle exceptions to ensure that your application behaves gracefully in case of errors. JDBC methods can throw `SQLException` and other exceptions, so it's essential to use try-catch blocks to catch and handle these exceptions.

```
try {
    // JDBC code that may throw exceptions
} catch (SQLException e) {
    // Handle database-related exceptions
    e.printStackTrace();
} finally {
    // Close resources in the finally block
    try {
        if (resultSet != null) {
            resultSet.close();
        }
        if (statement != null) {
            statement.close();
        }
        if (connection != null) {
            connection.close();
        }
    } catch (SQLException e) {
        e.printStackTrace();
    }
}
```

Executing SQL queries and updates in Java using JDBC is a fundamental skill for database-driven applications. Whether you're retrieving data for display or modifying database records, JDBC provides a reliable and secure way to interact with databases from your Java applications. By following best practices for error handling and resource management, you can ensure the robustness and reliability of your database operations.

7.3 Handling Result Sets

In the previous section, we discussed how to execute SQL queries and retrieve data using JDBC. Once a query is executed, the result is typically returned as a `ResultSet` object. In this section, we'll explore how to handle and work with `ResultSet` objects in Java.

Retrieving Data from a ResultSet

A `ResultSet` represents a set of rows and columns containing the data retrieved from a database query. To access the data within a `ResultSet`, you can use methods like `getInt()`, `getString()`, `getDouble()`, and others, which correspond to the data types of the columns in the result set.

Here's an example of how to retrieve data from a `ResultSet`:

```
String sql = "SELECT * FROM employees";
ResultSet resultSet = statement.executeQuery(sql);

while (resultSet.next()) {
    int employeeId = resultSet.getInt("employee_id");
    String firstName = resultSet.getString("first_name");
    String lastName = resultSet.getString("last_name");
    double salary = resultSet.getDouble("salary");
    // Process the retrieved data
}
```

The `next()` method is used to move the cursor to the next row in the result set. Initially, the cursor is positioned before the first row, so calling `next()` for the first time moves it to the first row.

Checking for NULL Values

You can use methods like `wasNull()` to check if a column value in the result set was NULL. For example:

```
String sql = "SELECT address FROM customers";
ResultSet resultSet = statement.executeQuery(sql);

while (resultSet.next()) {
    String address = resultSet.getString("address");
    if (resultSet.wasNull()) {
        // Handle NULL value
    }
}
```

Using Column Indices

In addition to using column names, you can also access columns by their index in the result set. The index is 1-based, meaning the first column has an index of 1.

```java
int employeeId = resultSet.getInt(1); // Retrieves the first column
String firstName = resultSet.getString(2); // Retrieves the second column
```

ResultSet Metadata

You can obtain metadata about the result set using the ResultSetMetaData interface. This metadata includes information about the columns in the result set, such as column names, data types, and more.

```java
ResultSetMetaData metaData = resultSet.getMetaData();
int columnCount = metaData.getColumnCount();

for (int i = 1; i <= columnCount; i++) {
    String columnName = metaData.getColumnName(i);
    String columnType = metaData.getColumnTypeName(i);
    // Process column metadata
}
```

Closing Result Sets

After you've finished processing a ResultSet, it's essential to close it to release resources and avoid memory leaks. You should also close the associated Statement and Connection objects.

```java
resultSet.close();
statement.close();
connection.close();
```

Handling result sets in Java is a crucial part of database programming with JDBC. By effectively retrieving and processing data from result sets, you can work with the information retrieved from the database in your Java applications. Additionally, understanding the metadata associated with result sets allows you to work with different database schemas and adapt your code accordingly. Proper resource management, including closing result sets, is essential for efficient and reliable database interactions.

7.4 Prepared Statements and Transactions

In database programming with JDBC, prepared statements and transactions are powerful features that enhance the security, efficiency, and reliability of database operations. In this section, we'll explore the use of prepared statements and transactions in Java.

Prepared Statements

Prepared statements are a way to execute SQL queries with placeholders for input values. They offer several advantages over regular statements constructed by concatenating strings:

1. **Security:** Prepared statements help prevent SQL injection attacks by automatically escaping input values.

2. **Performance:** They can be compiled once and reused with different parameter values, improving performance.

3. **Readability:** Code with placeholders is more readable and maintainable.

To create a prepared statement, you can use the PreparedStatement interface:

```
String sql = "INSERT INTO employees (first_name, last_name) VALUES (?, ?)";
PreparedStatement preparedStatement = connection.prepareStatement(sql);
```

You can set parameter values for the placeholders using methods like setString(), setInt(), and setDouble():

```
preparedStatement.setString(1, "John");
preparedStatement.setString(2, "Doe");
```

Then, you can execute the prepared statement:

```
preparedStatement.executeUpdate();
```

Transactions

A transaction is a sequence of one or more SQL statements treated as a single unit of work. Transactions are essential for ensuring data integrity and consistency in a database. In JDBC, you can work with transactions using the Connection object.

Here's how to work with transactions:

1. **Starting a Transaction:** You can start a transaction by disabling auto-commit mode:

   ```
   connection.setAutoCommit(false);
   ```

   This means that any SQL statements you execute will not be committed to the database automatically.

2. **Committing a Transaction:** To commit a transaction and make the changes permanent, use the commit() method:

   ```
   connection.commit();
   ```

   This should be called after a series of successful SQL statements.

3. **Rolling Back a Transaction:** If an error occurs or you need to undo changes within a transaction, you can roll back the transaction:

```
connection.rollback();
```

This reverts any changes made within the transaction to the previous state.

4. **Enabling Auto-Commit:** To return to auto-commit mode, use:

```
connection.setAutoCommit(true);
```

Transaction Management Example

Here's an example of managing a transaction in JDBC:

```
try {
    connection.setAutoCommit(false); // Start a transaction
    // Execute SQL statements within the transaction
    // ...
    connection.commit(); // Commit the transaction
} catch (SQLException e) {
    connection.rollback(); // Rollback the transaction in case of an error
    e.printStackTrace();
} finally {
    connection.setAutoCommit(true); // Return to auto-commit mode
}
```

Transactions are essential when you need to ensure that a series of database operations either all succeed or all fail together. They help maintain the consistency of data in the database and prevent partial or incomplete changes.

In summary, prepared statements enhance security and performance by allowing you to work with placeholders, while transactions ensure data integrity and consistency by grouping SQL statements into atomic units of work that can be committed or rolled back as needed. These features are essential for robust and reliable database interactions in Java applications.

7.5 Advanced JDBC Topics

In this section, we'll explore some advanced topics related to JDBC (Java Database Connectivity) that can help you work with databases more efficiently and effectively in your Java applications.

Connection Pooling

Connection pooling is a technique used to manage and reuse database connections, improving performance and reducing the overhead of creating and closing connections for each database operation. Instead of creating a new connection every time, a pool of preestablished connections is maintained, and applications can request and release connections as needed.

Popular connection pooling libraries for Java include Apache Commons DBCP, HikariCP, and c3p0. These libraries provide configuration options for managing connection pools, including maximum connections, timeouts, and connection validation.

Here's a basic example of how to use HikariCP for connection pooling:

```
HikariConfig config = new HikariConfig();
config.setJdbcUrl("jdbc:mysql://localhost:3306/mydb");
config.setUsername("username");
config.setPassword("password");

HikariDataSource dataSource = new HikariDataSource(config);

// Obtain a connection from the pool
Connection connection = dataSource.getConnection();

// Use the connection for database operations

// Return the connection to the pool
connection.close();
```

Batch Processing

Batch processing is a technique that allows you to group multiple SQL statements into a single batch and execute them together. This can significantly improve performance when you need to insert, update, or delete a large number of records in a database.

Here's a basic example of how to use batch processing in JDBC:

```
String sql = "INSERT INTO employees (first_name, last_name) VALUES (?, ?)";
PreparedStatement preparedStatement = connection.prepareStatement(sql);

for (Employee employee : employeesList) {
    preparedStatement.setString(1, employee.getFirstName());
    preparedStatement.setString(2, employee.getLastName());
    preparedStatement.addBatch();
}

int[] batchResult = preparedStatement.executeBatch();
```

In this example, we add multiple INSERT statements to the batch and execute them in a single call to executeBatch(). The method returns an array of integers representing the update counts for each statement.

Stored Procedures

Stored procedures are precompiled SQL code that can be stored and executed on the database server. JDBC allows you to call and work with stored procedures from your Java application.

To call a stored procedure, you can use a `CallableStatement`:

```
String sql = "{call getEmployeeDetails(?, ?)}";
CallableStatement callableStatement = connection.prepareCall(sql);

callableStatement.setInt(1, employeeId);
callableStatement.registerOutParameter(2, Types.VARCHAR);

callableStatement.execute();

String employeeName = callableStatement.getString(2);
```

In this example, we call a stored procedure named `getEmployeeDetails` with an input parameter `employeeId` and an output parameter to retrieve the employee's name.

Connection and Statement Caching

Some JDBC drivers and libraries provide caching mechanisms for both database connections and prepared statements. Caching can further improve performance by reusing cached connections and statements when possible. It's essential to configure and use these features judiciously, as they can have a significant impact on resource usage.

These advanced topics in JDBC can help you optimize your database interactions and improve the performance and scalability of your Java applications. Whether you're dealing with connection pooling, batch processing, stored procedures, or caching, understanding these concepts will enable you to make informed decisions when designing and developing database-driven applications in Java.

Chapter 8: Networking and Web Services

8.1 Socket Programming in Java

Socket programming is a fundamental aspect of network communication in Java, allowing applications to communicate over a network using sockets. A socket represents an endpoint for sending and receiving data across a network, and Java provides robust support for socket-based communication through the java.net package.

Socket Basics

In Java, you can create sockets using two main classes: Socket and ServerSocket. Here's a brief overview of each:

- **Socket**: This class represents a client-side socket. It allows you to connect to a server and exchange data.

- **ServerSocket**: This class represents a server-side socket. It listens for incoming client connections and creates new sockets for each client.

Client-Side Socket Example

Here's a basic example of creating a client-side socket in Java:

```java
import java.io.*;
import java.net.*;

public class ClientExample {
    public static void main(String[] args) {
        try {
            // Create a socket and connect to a server
            Socket socket = new Socket("localhost", 8080);

            // Create input and output streams
            OutputStream outputStream = socket.getOutputStream();
            PrintWriter writer = new PrintWriter(outputStream, true);

            // Send data to the server
            writer.println("Hello, Server!");

            // Close the socket
            socket.close();
        } catch (IOException e) {
            e.printStackTrace();
        }
    }
}
```

Server-Side Socket Example

Here's a basic example of creating a server-side socket in Java:

```java
import java.io.*;
import java.net.*;

public class ServerExample {
    public static void main(String[] args) {
        try {
            // Create a server socket and bind it to a port
            ServerSocket serverSocket = new ServerSocket(8080);

            // Accept incoming client connections
            Socket clientSocket = serverSocket.accept();

            // Create input and output streams
            InputStream inputStream = clientSocket.getInputStream();
            BufferedReader reader = new BufferedReader(new InputStreamReader(
inputStream));

            // Read data from the client
            String data = reader.readLine();
            System.out.println("Received from client: " + data);

            // Close the client socket and server socket
            clientSocket.close();
            serverSocket.close();
        } catch (IOException e) {
            e.printStackTrace();
        }
    }
}
```

In the server-side example, the server socket listens on port 8080 and accepts incoming client connections. It then reads data from the client and prints it to the console.

Socket programming is the foundation for various network communication protocols such as HTTP, FTP, and more. Understanding how to create and use sockets in Java is essential for building networked applications and services. In the next sections, we'll explore more advanced topics in networking and web services with Java.

8.2 Working with URLs and HTTP

Working with URLs and HTTP is a common requirement in modern Java applications. Whether you're building a web crawler, a RESTful API client, or an HTTP server, Java provides libraries and classes to make these tasks manageable. In this section, we'll explore how to work with URLs and HTTP in Java.

URLs in Java

The `java.net.URL` class represents a Uniform Resource Locator (URL). You can use it to parse, construct, and manipulate URLs. Here's how you can create a URL object and retrieve information from it:

```java
import java.net.*;

public class URLExample {
    public static void main(String[] args) {
        try {
            // Create a URL object
            URL url = new URL("https://www.example.com/path/to/resource?param
=value");

            // Get various components of the URL
            String protocol = url.getProtocol(); // "https"
            String host = url.getHost(); // "www.example.com"
            int port = url.getPort(); // -1 (default port)
            String path = url.getPath(); // "/path/to/resource"
            String query = url.getQuery(); // "param=value"

            System.out.println("Protocol: " + protocol);
            System.out.println("Host: " + host);
            System.out.println("Port: " + port);
            System.out.println("Path: " + path);
            System.out.println("Query: " + query);
        } catch (MalformedURLException e) {
            e.printStackTrace();
        }
    }
}
```

HTTP Requests in Java

To send HTTP requests in Java, you can use the `java.net.HttpURLConnection` class. This class allows you to create HTTP connections, set request headers, send data, and receive responses. Here's a basic example of sending an HTTP GET request:

```java
import java.io.*;
import java.net.*;

public class HttpGetExample {
    public static void main(String[] args) {
        try {
            // Create a URL object
            URL url = new URL("https://api.example.com/data");
```

```java
            // Open an HTTP connection
            HttpURLConnection connection = (HttpURLConnection) url.openConnec
tion();

            // Set the request method to GET
            connection.setRequestMethod("GET");

            // Read the response
            BufferedReader reader = new BufferedReader(new InputStreamReader(
connection.getInputStream()));
            String line;
            StringBuilder response = new StringBuilder();
            while ((line = reader.readLine()) != null) {
                response.append(line);
            }
            reader.close();

            // Print the response
            System.out.println("HTTP Response:");
            System.out.println(response.toString());

            // Close the connection
            connection.disconnect();
        } catch (IOException e) {
            e.printStackTrace();
        }
    }
}
```

HTTP Libraries in Java

While HttpURLConnection is suitable for basic HTTP requests, you may prefer to use more powerful HTTP client libraries like Apache HttpClient, OkHttp, or the HttpClient module introduced in Java 11. These libraries provide advanced features like connection pooling, authentication, and support for handling various response formats (JSON, XML, etc.).

```java
// Example using Apache HttpClient
import org.apache.http.client.*;
import org.apache.http.client.methods.*;
import org.apache.http.impl.client.*;

public class HttpClientExample {
    public static void main(String[] args) {
        try {
            CloseableHttpClient httpClient = HttpClients.createDefault();
            HttpGet httpGet = new HttpGet("https://api.example.com/data");

            CloseableHttpResponse response = httpClient.execute(httpGet);
```

```
        // Handle the response...

        httpClient.close();
    } catch (Exception e) {
        e.printStackTrace();
    }
  }
}
```

Working with URLs and HTTP in Java is essential for interacting with web services, APIs, and remote resources. Whether you're building a web client or a server, these capabilities are crucial for modern Java applications.

8.3 Creating RESTful Web Services

RESTful web services are a popular architectural style for building web APIs that are scalable, maintainable, and easy to use. Java provides various libraries and frameworks for creating RESTful web services, and in this section, we'll explore the basics of building RESTful web services using Java.

JAX-RS (Java API for RESTful Web Services)

Java EE (Enterprise Edition) includes a standard API called JAX-RS that simplifies the creation of RESTful web services. JAX-RS provides annotations and classes for defining RESTful resources, mapping HTTP methods to Java methods, and handling requests and responses.

Here's a simple example of creating a RESTful web service using JAX-RS:

```
import javax.ws.rs.*;
import javax.ws.rs.core.*;

@Path("/hello")
public class HelloWorldResource {

    @GET
    @Produces(MediaType.TEXT_PLAIN)
    public String sayHello() {
        return "Hello, World!";
    }
}
```

In this example, we define a resource class HelloWorldResource with a single method annotated with @GET. This method responds to HTTP GET requests to the /hello path and produces plain text as the response.

Deploying JAX-RS Web Services

To deploy JAX-RS web services, you typically package them as a WAR (Web Application Archive) file and deploy them to a servlet container like Apache Tomcat, or you can use a Java EE application server like WildFly or GlassFish.

Spring Boot for RESTful Web Services

Another popular approach to building RESTful web services in Java is to use the Spring Boot framework. Spring Boot simplifies the development of RESTful APIs by providing features like auto-configuration, embedded web servers, and dependency injection.

Here's a basic example of creating a RESTful web service with Spring Boot:

```java
import org.springframework.boot.*;
import org.springframework.boot.autoconfigure.*;
import org.springframework.web.bind.annotation.*;

@RestController
@EnableAutoConfiguration
public class HelloWorldController {

    @RequestMapping("/hello")
    public String sayHello() {
        return "Hello, World!";
    }

    public static void main(String[] args) {
        SpringApplication.run(HelloWorldController.class, args);
    }
}
```

In this Spring Boot example, we define a controller class with a @RequestMapping annotation that maps the /hello URL path to the sayHello method. Spring Boot takes care of setting up the web server and handling requests.

Other REST Frameworks

Apart from JAX-RS and Spring Boot, there are other Java frameworks like Jersey, RESTeasy, and Dropwizard that provide tools and libraries for building RESTful web services. Your choice of framework may depend on your project's requirements and familiarity with the framework's ecosystem.

Building RESTful web services in Java is a crucial skill for web developers and backend engineers. Whether you choose JAX-RS, Spring Boot, or another framework, understanding the principles of REST and how to expose and consume RESTful APIs is essential for modern web application development.

8.4 Consuming Web Services

Consuming web services is a common requirement in many Java applications, especially when you need to interact with external APIs or retrieve data from remote servers. Java provides various libraries and approaches for consuming web services, and in this section, we'll explore the basics of how to do it.

Java Libraries for Consuming Web Services

1. **HttpURLConnection:** Java's standard library includes the `java.net.HttpURLConnection` class, which can be used to make HTTP requests to web services. It's suitable for basic scenarios but lacks some advanced features found in other libraries.

2. **Apache HttpClient:** Apache HttpClient is a widely used library for making HTTP requests and consuming web services. It provides features like connection pooling, request and response interception, and support for various authentication methods.

3. **OkHttp:** OkHttp is a modern, efficient HTTP client for Java, which is known for its simplicity and performance. It's easy to use and provides features like connection pooling, automatic retries, and caching.

Example: Consuming a RESTful Web Service with HttpURLConnection

Here's a simple example of using `HttpURLConnection` to consume a RESTful web service:

```java
import java.io.*;
import java.net.*;

public class WebServiceConsumer {
    public static void main(String[] args) {
        try {
            // Create a URL object for the web service endpoint
            URL url = new URL("https://api.example.com/data");

            // Open an HTTP connection
            HttpURLConnection connection = (HttpURLConnection) url.openConnection();

            // Set the request method to GET
            connection.setRequestMethod("GET");

            // Read the response
            BufferedReader reader = new BufferedReader(new InputStreamReader(connection.getInputStream()));
            String line;
            StringBuilder response = new StringBuilder();
            while ((line = reader.readLine()) != null) {
```

```java
                response.append(line);
            }
            reader.close();

            // Print the response
            System.out.println("HTTP Response:");
            System.out.println(response.toString());

            // Close the connection
            connection.disconnect();
        } catch (IOException e) {
            e.printStackTrace();
        }
    }
}
```

Example: Consuming a RESTful Web Service with Apache HttpClient

Here's an example of using Apache HttpClient to consume a RESTful web service:

```java
import org.apache.http.client.*;
import org.apache.http.client.methods.*;
import org.apache.http.impl.client.*;

public class HttpClientConsumer {
    public static void main(String[] args) {
        try {
            CloseableHttpClient httpClient = HttpClients.createDefault();
            HttpGet httpGet = new HttpGet("https://api.example.com/data");

            CloseableHttpResponse response = httpClient.execute(httpGet);

            // Read and handle the response...

            httpClient.close();
        } catch (Exception e) {
            e.printStackTrace();
        }
    }
}
```

Consuming web services is a fundamental part of building modern Java applications that integrate with external services and APIs. Depending on your project's requirements and preferences, you can choose the appropriate library for making HTTP requests and handling web service responses.

8.5 Java RMI (Remote Method Invocation)

Java Remote Method Invocation (RMI) is a technology that allows Java objects to invoke methods on objects residing in other JVMs (Java Virtual Machines), possibly on different physical machines. RMI enables distributed computing and is commonly used in Java for building distributed systems and remote services.

How RMI Works

The basic idea behind RMI is to make a method of a remote object appear as if it were a local method invocation. This is achieved through the following components:

1. **Remote Interface:** A Java interface that declares the methods that can be invoked remotely. This interface must extend the `java.rmi.Remote` marker interface and declare that it throws `java.rmi.RemoteException`.

2. **Remote Object:** A Java class that implements the remote interface. This class defines the actual behavior of the remote methods.

3. **RMI Registry:** A registry service that keeps track of remote objects' references. Clients can look up these references in the registry to obtain a stub (proxy) that allows them to invoke remote methods.

4. **Stubs and Skeletons:** When you compile a remote interface, the RMI compiler (`rmic`) generates a stub and skeleton for each remote object. The stub is used by the client to make remote method calls, and the skeleton is used by the server to dispatch method invocations.

Example of Java RMI

Here's a simplified example of using Java RMI to create a remote service:

```java
// Remote interface
import java.rmi.*;

public interface MyRemoteInterface extends Remote {
    String sayHello() throws RemoteException;
}

// Remote object
import java.rmi.*;
import java.rmi.server.*;

public class MyRemoteObject extends UnicastRemoteObject implements MyRemoteIn
terface {
    public MyRemoteObject() throws RemoteException {
        // Constructor
    }
```

```java
    public String sayHello() throws RemoteException {
        return "Hello, from the remote server!";
    }
}

// Server
import java.rmi.*;

public class MyRMIServer {
    public static void main(String[] args) {
        try {
            MyRemoteInterface remoteObject = new MyRemoteObject();
            Naming.rebind("MyRemoteObject", remoteObject);
            System.out.println("Server is ready.");
        } catch (Exception e) {
            e.printStackTrace();
        }
    }
}

// Client
import java.rmi.*;

public class MyRMIClient {
    public static void main(String[] args) {
        try {
            MyRemoteInterface remoteObject = (MyRemoteInterface) Naming.looku
p("rmi://localhost/MyRemoteObject");
            String message = remoteObject.sayHello();
            System.out.println("Message from server: " + message);
        } catch (Exception e) {
            e.printStackTrace();
        }
    }
}
```

In this example:

- MyRemoteInterface declares the remote method sayHello.
- MyRemoteObject implements MyRemoteInterface and provides the actual implementation of sayHello.
- The server (MyRMIServer) creates an instance of MyRemoteObject, binds it to the RMI registry, and makes it available for remote invocations.
- The client (MyRMIClient) looks up the remote object in the registry and invokes the sayHello method.

Java RMI is a powerful technology for building distributed Java applications. It simplifies remote method invocation and allows you to design distributed systems in a way that makes remote method calls feel like local method calls.

Chapter 9: Java Design Patterns

9.1 Introduction to Design Patterns

Design patterns are reusable solutions to common problems that software developers encounter during the design and development of software applications. They provide a structured approach to solving design and coding issues, making it easier to create maintainable, scalable, and flexible code.

Why Use Design Patterns?

Design patterns offer several advantages:

1. **Reusability:** Design patterns encapsulate best practices and can be reused across different projects. This reduces the need to reinvent the wheel for solving common problems.

2. **Maintainability:** Patterns promote clean and organized code, making it easier to understand, modify, and maintain.

3. **Scalability:** Patterns help create flexible and extensible software designs, allowing applications to evolve over time without major rework.

4. **Communication:** Design patterns provide a common vocabulary for developers to discuss and communicate about software designs.

Types of Design Patterns

Design patterns can be categorized into three main types:

1. **Creational Patterns:** These patterns focus on object creation mechanisms, providing flexibility in object instantiation. Examples include Singleton, Factory Method, and Abstract Factory.

2. **Structural Patterns:** Structural patterns deal with object composition and help define how objects can be combined to form larger structures. Examples include Adapter, Decorator, and Composite.

3. **Behavioral Patterns:** Behavioral patterns address how objects interact and communicate with each other. They define the responsibilities and interactions between objects. Examples include Observer, Strategy, and Command.

Example: Singleton Pattern

The Singleton pattern ensures that a class has only one instance and provides a global point of access to that instance. Here's an example of a Singleton pattern implementation in Java:

```java
public class Singleton {
    // Private constructor to prevent instantiation from other classes
    private Singleton() {}

    // Private static instance of the class
    private static Singleton instance;

    // Public method to provide access to the instance
    public static Singleton getInstance() {
        if (instance == null) {
            instance = new Singleton();
        }
        return instance;
    }
}
```

In this example, the Singleton class has a private constructor to prevent direct instantiation, and the getInstance method provides the only way to access the Singleton instance. This ensures that there's only one instance of the Singleton class throughout the application.

Design patterns are an essential part of software engineering, and they provide solutions to recurring design problems. Understanding and applying design patterns can significantly improve the quality and maintainability of your Java applications. In the following sections, we'll explore various design patterns in Java and their practical applications.

9.2 Creational Patterns

Creational design patterns deal with object creation mechanisms, attempting to create objects in a manner suitable to the situation. They provide flexibility in object creation and help make a system independent of how its objects are created, composed, and represented. In Java, several creational design patterns are commonly used to create objects. Here, we'll explore some of the key creational patterns:

1. Singleton Pattern

The Singleton pattern ensures that a class has only one instance and provides a global point of access to that instance. It's useful when you want to control access to a shared resource, such as a database connection or a configuration manager.

Here's a simple example of a Singleton implementation in Java:

```java
public class Singleton {
    private static Singleton instance;

    private Singleton() {
        // Private constructor to prevent instantiation
    }
```

```java
    public static Singleton getInstance() {
        if (instance == null) {
            instance = new Singleton();
        }
        return instance;
    }
}
```

2. Factory Method Pattern

The Factory Method pattern defines an interface for creating an object but allows subclasses to alter the type of objects that will be created. It provides an interface for creating objects but leaves the choice of the concrete class to the subclasses.

```java
public interface Product {
    void create();
}

public class ConcreteProductA implements Product {
    public void create() {
        System.out.println("Creating Product A");
    }
}

public class ConcreteProductB implements Product {
    public void create() {
        System.out.println("Creating Product B");
    }
}

public interface Creator {
    Product factoryMethod();
}

public class ConcreteCreatorA implements Creator {
    public Product factoryMethod() {
        return new ConcreteProductA();
    }
}

public class ConcreteCreatorB implements Creator {
    public Product factoryMethod() {
        return new ConcreteProductB();
    }
}
```

3. Abstract Factory Pattern

The Abstract Factory pattern provides an interface for creating families of related or dependent objects without specifying their concrete classes. It's useful when you need to ensure that the created objects are compatible with each other.

```java
public interface Button {
    void render();
}

public interface Checkbox {
    void render();
}

public interface GUIFactory {
    Button createButton();
    Checkbox createCheckbox();
}

public class WindowsFactory implements GUIFactory {
    public Button createButton() {
        return new WindowsButton();
    }

    public Checkbox createCheckbox() {
        return new WindowsCheckbox();
    }
}

public class MacOSFactory implements GUIFactory {
    public Button createButton() {
        return new MacOSButton();
    }

    public Checkbox createCheckbox() {
        return new MacOSCheckbox();
    }
}
```

4. Builder Pattern

The Builder pattern separates the construction of a complex object from its representation, allowing the same construction process to create different representations. It's particularly useful when an object has a large number of optional attributes.

```java
public class Meal {
    private String mainCourse;
    private String side;
    private String drink;
```

```java
    // Getters and setters...

    @Override
    public String toString() {
        return "Meal [mainCourse=" + mainCourse + ", side=" + side + ", drink
=" + drink + "]";
    }
}

public interface MealBuilder {
    void buildMainCourse();
    void buildSide();
    void buildDrink();
    Meal getMeal();
}

public class VegMealBuilder implements MealBuilder {
    private Meal meal = new Meal();

    public void buildMainCourse() {
        meal.setMainCourse("Vegetarian Burger");
    }

    public void buildSide() {
        meal.setSide("Fries");
    }

    public void buildDrink() {
        meal.setDrink("Coke");
    }

    public Meal getMeal() {
        return meal;
    }
}
```

These are just a few examples of creational design patterns in Java. Each pattern addresses specific concerns related to object creation, allowing you to design your software in a more flexible and maintainable way. When choosing a creational pattern, consider the requirements of your application and the benefits each pattern provides.

9.3 Structural Patterns

Structural design patterns focus on how classes and objects are composed to form larger structures. They help define the relationships between objects, making it easier to manage object composition. In Java, several structural design patterns are commonly used to solve design problems. Here, we'll explore some of the key structural patterns:

1. Adapter Pattern

The Adapter pattern allows the interface of an existing class to be used as another interface. It's often used to make existing classes work with others without modifying their source code.

```java
// Adaptee (existing class)
public class OldSystem {
    public void doLegacyThing() {
        System.out.println("Doing legacy thing...");
    }
}

// Target interface
public interface NewSystem {
    void doNewThing();
}

// Adapter
public class Adapter implements NewSystem {
    private OldSystem legacySystem;

    public Adapter(OldSystem legacySystem) {
        this.legacySystem = legacySystem;
    }

    public void doNewThing() {
        legacySystem.doLegacyThing();
    }
}
```

2. Decorator Pattern

The Decorator pattern allows you to add behavior or responsibilities to individual objects, either statically or dynamically, without affecting the behavior of other objects from the same class.

```java
// Component interface
public interface Coffee {
    double getCost();
    String getDescription();
}

// Concrete component
public class SimpleCoffee implements Coffee {
    public double getCost() {
        return 2.0;
    }

    public String getDescription() {
```

```java
        return "Simple Coffee";
    }
}

// Decorator
public abstract class CoffeeDecorator implements Coffee {
    protected final Coffee decoratedCoffee;

    public CoffeeDecorator(Coffee decoratedCoffee) {
        this.decoratedCoffee = decoratedCoffee;
    }
}

// Concrete decorators
public class MilkDecorator extends CoffeeDecorator {
    public MilkDecorator(Coffee decoratedCoffee) {
        super(decoratedCoffee);
    }

    public double getCost() {
        return decoratedCoffee.getCost() + 0.5;
    }

    public String getDescription() {
        return decoratedCoffee.getDescription() + ", Milk";
    }
}
```

3. Composite Pattern

The Composite pattern allows you to compose objects into tree structures to represent part-whole hierarchies. It treats individual objects and compositions of objects uniformly.

```java
// Component interface
public interface Graphic {
    void draw();
}

// Leaf
public class Circle implements Graphic {
    public void draw() {
        System.out.println("Drawing a circle");
    }
}

// Composite
public class CompositeGraphic implements Graphic {
    private List<Graphic> graphics = new ArrayList<>();

    public void addGraphic(Graphic graphic) {
```

```
        graphics.add(graphic);
    }

    public void draw() {
        for (Graphic graphic : graphics) {
            graphic.draw();
        }
    }
}
```

4. Proxy Pattern

The Proxy pattern provides a surrogate or placeholder for another object to control access to it. It's useful for scenarios such as lazy initialization, access control, or monitoring.

```
// Subject interface
public interface Image {
    void display();
}

// Real subject
public class RealImage implements Image {
    private String filename;

    public RealImage(String filename) {
        this.filename = filename;
        loadFromDisk();
    }

    private void loadFromDisk() {
        System.out.println("Loading image: " + filename);
    }

    public void display() {
        System.out.println("Displaying image: " + filename);
    }
}

// Proxy
public class ImageProxy implements Image {
    private RealImage realImage;
    private String filename;

    public ImageProxy(String filename) {
        this.filename = filename;
    }

    public void display() {
        if (realImage == null) {
            realImage = new RealImage(filename);
```

```
        }
        realImage.display();
    }
}
```

These structural design patterns in Java provide solutions to organizing and managing objects in your application. They allow you to create complex structures while keeping your code flexible and maintainable. When choosing a structural pattern, consider the relationships between objects and how they can be composed to meet your design goals.

9.4 Behavioral Patterns

Behavioral design patterns in Java focus on how objects interact and communicate with each other. They address the responsibilities and behaviors of objects within a system. These patterns help define the collaboration between objects, making it easier to understand and manage the flow of control in your application. Let's explore some important behavioral design patterns in Java:

1. Observer Pattern

The Observer pattern defines a one-to-many dependency between objects, so that when one object changes state, all its dependents are notified and updated automatically. It's commonly used in event handling systems and UI components.

```java
// Observer interface
public interface Observer {
    void update(String message);
}

// Concrete Observer
public class ConcreteObserver implements Observer {
    private String name;

    public ConcreteObserver(String name) {
        this.name = name;
    }

    public void update(String message) {
        System.out.println(name + " received message: " + message);
    }
}

// Subject (Observable) interface
import java.util.ArrayList;
import java.util.List;

public interface Subject {
```

```java
    void addObserver(Observer observer);
    void removeObserver(Observer observer);
    void notifyObservers(String message);
}

// Concrete Subject (Observable)
public class ConcreteSubject implements Subject {
    private List<Observer> observers = new ArrayList<>();

    public void addObserver(Observer observer) {
        observers.add(observer);
    }

    public void removeObserver(Observer observer) {
        observers.remove(observer);
    }

    public void notifyObservers(String message) {
        for (Observer observer : observers) {
            observer.update(message);
        }
    }
}
```

2. Strategy Pattern

The Strategy pattern defines a family of algorithms, encapsulates each one, and makes them interchangeable. It allows you to choose the appropriate algorithm at runtime without altering the client code.

```java
// Strategy interface
public interface PaymentStrategy {
    void pay(int amount);
}

// Concrete Strategies
public class CreditCardPayment implements PaymentStrategy {
    private String cardNumber;

    public CreditCardPayment(String cardNumber) {
        this.cardNumber = cardNumber;
    }

    public void pay(int amount) {
        System.out.println("Paid " + amount + " via credit card " + cardNumbe
r);
    }
}
```

```java
public class PayPalPayment implements PaymentStrategy {
    private String email;

    public PayPalPayment(String email) {
        this.email = email;
    }

    public void pay(int amount) {
        System.out.println("Paid " + amount + " via PayPal to " + email);
    }
}

// Context
public class ShoppingCart {
    private PaymentStrategy paymentStrategy;

    public void setPaymentStrategy(PaymentStrategy paymentStrategy) {
        this.paymentStrategy = paymentStrategy;
    }

    public void checkout(int amount) {
        paymentStrategy.pay(amount);
    }
}
```

3. Command Pattern

The Command pattern encapsulates a request as an object, thereby allowing you to parameterize clients with queues, requests, and operations. It also enables you to support undoable operations.

```java
// Command interface
public interface Command {
    void execute();
}

// Receiver
public class Light {
    public void turnOn() {
        System.out.println("Light is on");
    }

    public void turnOff() {
        System.out.println("Light is off");
    }
}

// Concrete Commands
public class TurnOnLightCommand implements Command {
```

```java
    private Light light;

    public TurnOnLightCommand(Light light) {
        this.light = light;
    }

    public void execute() {
        light.turnOn();
    }
}

public class TurnOffLightCommand implements Command {
    private Light light;

    public TurnOffLightCommand(Light light) {
        this.light = light;
    }

    public void execute() {
        light.turnOff();
    }
}

// Invoker
public class RemoteControl {
    private Command command;

    public void setCommand(Command command) {
        this.command = command;
    }

    public void pressButton() {
        command.execute();
    }
}
```

4. Chain of Responsibility Pattern

The Chain of Responsibility pattern passes a request along a chain of handlers. Each handler decides either to process the request or pass it to the next handler in the chain. It promotes loose coupling between senders and receivers of requests.

```java
// Handler interface
public abstract class Handler {
    protected Handler successor;

    public void setSuccessor(Handler successor) {
        this.successor = successor;
    }
}
```

```java
    public abstract void handleRequest(Request request);
}

// Concrete Handlers
public class ConcreteHandler1 extends Handler {
    public void handleRequest(Request request) {
        if (request.getType() == RequestType.TYPE1) {
            System.out.println("Handled request of Type1");
        } else if (successor != null) {
            successor.handleRequest(request);
        }
    }
}

public class ConcreteHandler2 extends Handler {
    public void handleRequest(Request request) {
        if (request.getType() == RequestType.TYPE2) {
            System.out.println("Handled request of Type2");
        } else if (successor != null) {
            successor.handleRequest(request);
        }
    }
}

// Request and RequestType enums
public class Request {
    private RequestType type;

    public Request(RequestType type) {
        this.type = type;
    }

    public RequestType getType() {
        return type;
    }
}

public enum RequestType {
    TYPE1, TYPE2, TYPE3
}
```

These behavioral design patterns in Java help you manage the interactions and responsibilities of objects in a flexible and maintainable way. They promote good design practices by separating concerns and allowing you to make changes to individual components without affecting the entire system. When implementing these patterns, consider the specific requirements of your application to choose the most appropriate one.

9.5 Real-World Application of Design Patterns

Design patterns are powerful tools for solving common software design problems. In this section, we'll explore some real-world scenarios where design patterns can be applied to improve the structure, maintainability, and scalability of Java applications.

1. Singleton Pattern

The Singleton pattern ensures that a class has only one instance and provides a global point of access to that instance. It's useful in scenarios where you need to control access to shared resources, such as a configuration manager or a connection pool.

```java
public class DatabaseConnection {
    private static DatabaseConnection instance;

    private DatabaseConnection() {
        // Private constructor to prevent instantiation
    }

    public static DatabaseConnection getInstance() {
        if (instance == null) {
            instance = new DatabaseConnection();
        }
        return instance;
    }

    public void connect() {
        // Connect to the database
    }
}
```

2. Factory Method Pattern

The Factory Method pattern allows you to create objects without specifying the exact class of object that will be created. It's commonly used in frameworks and libraries where you want to delegate the responsibility of object creation to subclasses.

```java
public abstract class Logger {
    public abstract void log(String message);
}

public class ConsoleLogger extends Logger {
    public void log(String message) {
        System.out.println("Console Log: " + message);
    }
}

public class FileLogger extends Logger {
```

```java
    public void log(String message) {
        // Log to a file
    }
}

public interface LoggerFactory {
    Logger createLogger();
}

public class ConsoleLoggerFactory implements LoggerFactory {
    public Logger createLogger() {
        return new ConsoleLogger();
    }
}

public class FileLoggerFactory implements LoggerFactory {
    public Logger createLogger() {
        return new FileLogger();
    }
}
```

3. Observer Pattern

The Observer pattern is widely used in event-driven systems and user interfaces. It allows multiple objects to listen for and react to changes in the state of another object. For example, in a stock trading application, multiple clients (observers) can subscribe to updates from a stock market feed (subject) and react accordingly.

```java
// Observer interface
public interface StockObserver {
    void update(String stockSymbol, double price);
}

// Concrete Observer
public class StockTrader implements StockObserver {
    private String name;

    public StockTrader(String name) {
        this.name = name;
    }

    public void update(String stockSymbol, double price) {
        // Implement trading strategy based on stock price updates
    }
}

// Subject
public class StockMarket {
    private List<StockObserver> observers = new ArrayList<>();
```

```java
    public void addObserver(StockObserver observer) {
        observers.add(observer);
    }

    public void removeObserver(StockObserver observer) {
        observers.remove(observer);
    }

    public void notifyObservers(String stockSymbol, double price) {
        for (StockObserver observer : observers) {
            observer.update(stockSymbol, price);
        }
    }
}
```

These are just a few examples of how design patterns can be applied to solve real-world problems in Java applications. Design patterns provide a common language and set of best practices for software developers, making it easier to understand and collaborate on complex systems. When faced with a specific design challenge, it's essential to choose the most appropriate design pattern to address the problem effectively.

Chapter 10: Unit Testing and Debugging

10.1 Writing JUnit Tests

JUnit is a popular framework for writing and running unit tests in Java. Unit testing is a critical part of the software development process, as it helps ensure that individual components or units of code work correctly in isolation. In this section, we will explore how to write JUnit tests to verify the behavior of your Java classes and methods.

Writing Your First JUnit Test

Let's start with a simple example. Suppose you have a class called `Calculator` with a method add that adds two numbers. You want to write a JUnit test to ensure that the add method works as expected.

```java
import org.junit.jupiter.api.Test;
import static org.junit.jupiter.api.Assertions.*;

public class CalculatorTest {

    @Test
    public void testAdd() {
        // Arrange: Create an instance of the Calculator class
        Calculator calculator = new Calculator();

        // Act: Call the add method
        int result = calculator.add(2, 3);

        // Assert: Check if the result is as expected
        assertEquals(5, result);
    }
}
```

In this test case, we use JUnit's annotations. The `@Test` annotation indicates that the `testAdd` method is a test case. Inside the test case, we arrange by creating an instance of the `Calculator` class, act by calling the add method with arguments 2 and 3, and finally assert by checking if the result is equal to 5 using `assertEquals`.

Running JUnit Tests

To run JUnit tests, you can use your IDE's built-in test runner or use a build tool like Maven or Gradle. Most modern IDEs provide a convenient way to run JUnit tests and display the results in a user-friendly format.

Assertions in JUnit

JUnit provides a variety of assertion methods in the org.junit.jupiter.api.Assertions class. These methods allow you to check conditions and ensure that your code behaves correctly. Here are some commonly used assertions:

- assertEquals(expected, actual): Checks if the expected value is equal to the actual value.
- assertTrue(condition): Checks if the condition is true.
- assertFalse(condition): Checks if the condition is false.
- assertNull(object): Checks if the object is null.
- assertNotNull(object): Checks if the object is not null.

Testing Exception Handling

You can also write tests to ensure that your methods throw the correct exceptions when expected. Use the assertThrows method to accomplish this:

```
@Test
public void testDivideByZero() {
    Calculator calculator = new Calculator();

    assertThrows(ArithmeticException.class, () -> {
        calculator.divide(5, 0);
    });
}
```

In this example, we expect the divide method to throw an ArithmeticException when dividing by zero.

Organizing Test Cases

It's essential to organize your test cases effectively. You can group related test cases into test suites and use test fixtures to set up common test conditions.

JUnit provides annotations like @BeforeAll, @BeforeEach, @AfterEach, and @AfterAll to manage test fixtures and setup/teardown operations.

Best Practices for Unit Testing

- Write tests early in the development process.
- Keep your tests independent and isolated from each other.
- Test both expected and unexpected inputs.
- Use meaningful test method and class names.
- Continuously refactor and maintain your tests as your code evolves.

JUnit is a versatile and widely adopted tool for unit testing in Java, and mastering it will help you ensure the correctness of your code as your project grows in complexity. In the following sections, we'll explore more advanced topics in unit testing, including test-driven development (TDD) and debugging Java applications.

10.2 Test-Driven Development (TDD)

Test-Driven Development (TDD) is a software development methodology that emphasizes writing tests before writing the actual code. The primary goal of TDD is to ensure that your code is correct and reliable by design, right from the start of development. This section explores the principles and practices of TDD in the context of Java development.

The TDD Cycle

TDD follows a repetitive cycle known as the "Red-Green-Refactor" cycle:

1. **Red**: Write a failing test case that defines the behavior you want to implement. At this stage, your test should fail because the code it's testing doesn't exist yet.

2. **Green**: Write the minimum amount of code necessary to make the failing test case pass. Your goal is to make the test case succeed, not to write perfect or complete code.

3. **Refactor**: Once the test case passes, refactor your code to improve its structure, readability, and performance while keeping all tests passing. Refactoring is a crucial step to maintain the quality of your codebase.

Example of TDD in Java

Let's illustrate TDD with a simple example. Suppose you're developing a class called MathUtils, and you want to implement a method called multiply. You would start with a failing test case:

```java
import org.junit.jupiter.api.Test;
import static org.junit.jupiter.api.Assertions.*;

public class MathUtilsTest {

    @Test
    public void testMultiply() {
        MathUtils mathUtils = new MathUtils();
        assertEquals(10, mathUtils.multiply(2, 5));
    }
}
```

At this point, the multiply method doesn't exist in the MathUtils class, so the test fails.

Next, you would implement the multiply method to make the test pass:

```java
public class MathUtils {
    public int multiply(int a, int b) {
```

```
        return a * b;
    }
}
```

Now, when you run the test, it should pass, indicating that your implementation is correct for this specific case.

TDD offers several benefits to developers and the development process:

1. **Improved Code Quality**: TDD encourages writing clean, modular, and well-tested code, resulting in higher-quality software.

2. **Early Detection of Issues**: By writing tests first, you catch bugs and design flaws early in the development cycle, reducing the cost of fixing issues later.

3. **Documentation**: Tests serve as documentation for your code, helping others understand how your code is expected to behave.

4. **Confidence**: TDD gives you confidence that your code works correctly, even as you make changes and enhancements.

5. **Supports Refactoring**: TDD makes it safer and easier to refactor your code because you have tests in place to verify that your changes don't introduce regressions.

6. **Reduces Debugging Time**: Since you catch issues early and have a suite of tests, you spend less time debugging.

To effectively practice TDD in Java or any programming language, consider the following best practices:

- Start with simple, small tests.
- Write tests that focus on a single behavior or requirement.
- Refactor your code after each passing test to improve its quality.
- Automate your test suite to run frequently.
- Maintain a balance between writing production code and tests.

TDD can be a powerful approach to developing reliable and maintainable Java applications. It promotes a mindset where testing becomes an integral part of the development process, leading to better software quality and more efficient development.

10.3 Debugging Java Applications

Debugging is a crucial skill for developers. It involves identifying and fixing issues in your code to ensure that it works as intended. This section explores various debugging techniques and tools available for Java developers.

Debugging Techniques

1. *Print Statements:*
   - One of the simplest debugging techniques is to insert print statements in your code to output variable values, method calls, or other information at specific points in your code.
   - Use `System.out.println()` or a logging framework like Log4j to print messages to the console or log files.
   - This approach is effective for identifying the flow of your program and the values of variables but can be time-consuming and may clutter your code.

2. *Interactive Debugging:*
   - Java provides a powerful tool for interactive debugging through Integrated Development Environments (IDEs) like Eclipse, IntelliJ IDEA, or NetBeans.
   - You can set breakpoints in your code, run your application in debug mode, and then step through the code line by line, inspecting variables and their values.
   - This allows you to pinpoint the exact location of issues and understand the state of your program at each step.

3. *Exception Handling:*
   - Proper exception handling is essential for identifying and handling errors in your code.
   - Utilize try-catch blocks to catch and handle exceptions gracefully.
   - Logging exceptions or printing stack traces can help you understand the cause of errors.

4. *Logging:*
   - Use logging frameworks like Log4j, Logback, or Java's built-in `java.util.logging` to record events and errors in your application.
   - Logging provides a detailed history of what your program is doing, which can be invaluable for debugging issues in production.

5. *Unit Testing:*
   - Unit tests can serve as a form of debugging by helping you catch and fix issues early in the development process.
   - Writing comprehensive unit tests ensures that individual components of your code work as expected, reducing the need for extensive debugging later.

Debugging Tools

1. Integrated Development Environments (IDEs):
- IDEs like Eclipse, IntelliJ IDEA, and NetBeans provide robust debugging capabilities.
- They offer features such as setting breakpoints, inspecting variables, evaluating expressions, and stepping through code.

2. Command-Line Debugging:
- The Java Virtual Machine (JVM) offers command-line debugging options using the jdb (Java Debugger) tool.
- While not as user-friendly as IDEs, it allows you to debug Java applications from the command line.

3. Profiling Tools:
- Profiling tools like VisualVM, YourKit, and Java Mission Control help identify performance bottlenecks and memory issues in your Java applications.
- Profilers provide insights into CPU and memory usage, thread behavior, and more.

4. Remote Debugging:
- You can debug Java applications remotely by connecting an IDE to a running Java process on a different machine.
- This is useful for debugging applications in production or on remote servers.

Best Practices for Debugging

To be effective at debugging Java applications, consider these best practices:

- **Reproduce the Issue**: Before debugging, try to reproduce the issue consistently. Understanding the conditions under which it occurs is crucial.
- **Start with Logs**: Review logs and error messages to gather initial information about the problem.
- **Isolate the Issue**: Narrow down the problem to a specific component or area of your code.
- **Use Version Control**: If you have version control in place (e.g., Git), create a separate branch for debugging to avoid disrupting the main codebase.
- **Document Findings**: Keep track of your debugging process, including the steps you've taken and any insights gained.
- **Fix One Issue at a Time**: Avoid making multiple changes simultaneously. Fix one issue, test it, and move on to the next.
- **Know When to Seek Help**: If you're stuck and unable to solve an issue, don't hesitate to seek help from colleagues or online communities.

Debugging is an essential skill for Java developers, and mastering it will greatly enhance your ability to create reliable and maintainable Java applications. Whether you use print statements, sophisticated IDEs, or profiling tools, the goal is to identify and resolve issues efficiently.

10.4 Profiling and Performance Tuning

Profiling and performance tuning are essential aspects of Java development. They involve identifying bottlenecks and optimizing your code to ensure it runs efficiently. In this section, we'll explore profiling tools, performance optimization techniques, and best practices for improving the performance of your Java applications.

Profiling Tools

Profiling tools help you analyze the runtime behavior of your Java applications. They provide insights into CPU usage, memory allocation, thread activity, and more. Some popular profiling tools for Java include:

1. **VisualVM**: VisualVM is a free and powerful profiling and performance analysis tool that comes bundled with the Java Development Kit (JDK). It offers features like CPU profiling, heap dump analysis, and thread monitoring.

2. **YourKit**: YourKit Java Profiler is a commercial profiler known for its low overhead and deep insights into application performance. It provides memory and CPU profiling, thread analysis, and database profiling.

3. **Java Mission Control**: Java Mission Control is part of the Oracle JDK and offers a set of tools for performance monitoring, profiling, and diagnostics. It includes Flight Recorder for continuous monitoring and analysis.

4. **Profiler Plugins**: Many Integrated Development Environments (IDEs), such as IntelliJ IDEA and Eclipse, offer profiling plugins that integrate with popular profilers, making it easier to profile your code within your development environment.

Profiling Process

Profiling typically involves the following steps:

1. **Identify Performance Goals**: Determine the specific performance goals you want to achieve, such as reducing CPU usage, improving response times, or optimizing memory usage.

2. **Instrument Your Code**: Use profiling tools to instrument your code, either by adding annotations or configuring the profiler to start collecting data when your application runs.

3. **Run the Profiler**: Execute your application with the profiler attached. Collect data on CPU usage, memory allocation, and other performance metrics while your application is in operation.

4. **Analyze the Data**: Use the profiler's graphical interface to analyze the collected data. Look for performance bottlenecks, excessive memory usage, and areas where CPU time is spent inefficiently.

5. **Optimize**: Based on the profiler's findings, make code changes to optimize the identified performance issues. This may involve refactoring, adjusting algorithms, or optimizing database queries.

6. **Repeat**: Profile your code again after making optimizations to ensure that your changes have improved performance as expected.

Performance Optimization Techniques

Here are some common techniques for optimizing the performance of Java applications:

1. **Use Efficient Data Structures**: Choose data structures that are well-suited to your application's needs. For example, use HashMaps for fast key-value lookups and ArrayLists for indexed access.

2. **Minimize Object Creation**: Excessive object creation can lead to increased memory usage and garbage collection overhead. Reuse objects when possible or use object pooling.

3. **Multithreading**: Utilize Java's multithreading capabilities to parallelize tasks and make use of multiple CPU cores. However, be mindful of synchronization overhead.

4. **Database Optimization**: Optimize database queries, use indexing, and consider caching strategies to reduce database access latency.

5. **Memory Management**: Monitor and manage memory usage carefully. Identify and eliminate memory leaks, and use memory profiling tools to analyze memory consumption.

6. **Algorithm Optimization**: Choose efficient algorithms and data structures for your specific tasks. Sometimes, a simple algorithm tweak can lead to significant performance improvements.

7. **Profiling-Based Optimization**: Focus on optimizing the parts of your code that profiling tools identify as performance bottlenecks.

8. **Batch Processing**: For applications that involve batch processing, optimize batch sizes and consider using bulk insert/update operations.

Best Practices

To effectively profile and optimize your Java applications, consider the following best practices:

- **Profile Early**: Start profiling early in the development process to catch performance issues before they become ingrained in your codebase.

- **Set Realistic Goals**: Define achievable performance goals and prioritize optimization efforts based on their impact on user experience.

- **Test Under Load**: Test your application under realistic load conditions to identify performance bottlenecks that may not be apparent in development.

- **Document Changes**: Document performance improvements and the reasoning behind them, as well as any trade-offs made during optimization.

- **Monitor in Production**: Continue monitoring your application's performance in production to catch issues that may arise under real-world conditions.

Profiling and performance tuning are ongoing processes that require careful analysis and continuous improvement. By investing time in these activities, you can ensure that your Java applications run efficiently and provide a better user experience.

10.5 Continuous Integration with Java

Continuous Integration (CI) is a development practice that involves regularly integrating code changes into a shared repository and automatically running tests and builds to detect integration issues early. In this section, we'll explore CI principles, tools, and best practices for Java development.

CI Principles

CI is based on several fundamental principles:

1. **Frequent Integration**: Developers integrate their code changes frequently, often multiple times a day, to avoid long-lived branches and reduce the risk of integration conflicts.

2. **Automated Testing**: Automated tests, including unit tests, integration tests, and end-to-end tests, are an essential part of CI. These tests are executed automatically after each code commit.

3. **Automated Builds**: CI tools automatically build the application from source code. This ensures that the codebase is always in a buildable state.

4. **Immediate Feedback**: Developers receive immediate feedback on the quality of their code changes. If a test fails or the build is broken, the team can address the issue promptly.

5. **Version Control**: CI relies on version control systems like Git to manage code changes and facilitate collaboration among team members.

CI Tools for Java

Several CI tools are well-suited for Java development:

1. **Jenkins**: Jenkins is a popular open-source CI/CD tool that supports Java. It offers a wide range of plugins for building, testing, and deploying Java applications.

2. **Travis CI**: Travis CI is a cloud-based CI service that integrates with GitHub repositories. It supports Java and provides a simple configuration file for defining the build process.

3. **CircleCI**: CircleCI is a cloud-based CI/CD platform that automates the software development process. It supports Java and offers flexibility in defining workflows.

4. **GitLab CI/CD**: GitLab provides built-in CI/CD capabilities and integrates seamlessly with GitLab repositories. You can define CI/CD pipelines for Java projects.

5. **GitHub Actions**: GitHub Actions allows you to automate workflows, including building and testing Java applications, directly within GitHub repositories.

Setting Up CI for Java

To set up CI for your Java project, follow these general steps:

1. **Choose a CI Tool**: Select a CI tool that fits your project's requirements and integrates well with your version control system.

2. **Create CI Configuration**: Create a configuration file (e.g., `.jenkinsfile`, `.travis.yml`, or `.circleci/config.yml`) that defines the CI workflow. Specify build steps, testing procedures, and deployment instructions.

3. **Integrate with Version Control**: Configure your CI tool to monitor your version control system for code changes. Most CI tools can be triggered automatically when code is pushed or merged.

4. **Automate Builds**: Set up automated build tasks that compile your Java code and package your application. Use build tools like Maven or Gradle.

5. **Automate Testing**: Configure automated testing, including running unit tests, integration tests, and any other relevant tests. CI tools can generate reports and notify you of test failures.

6. **Artifact Generation**: If your project produces artifacts (e.g., JAR files), make sure they are generated as part of the CI process.

7. **Deployment**: If your CI/CD pipeline includes deployment steps, ensure that deployment is automated and repeatable.

Best Practices

Here are some best practices for implementing CI with Java:

- **Keep Build Times Short**: Aim for fast build times by optimizing dependencies, using caching, and minimizing unnecessary tasks.

- **Isolate Dependencies**: Isolate dependencies for testing to ensure that CI tests don't rely on external resources or services.

- **Version Control**: Maintain a clear version control strategy and commit frequently. Use feature branches and pull requests for collaboration.

- **Use Containerization**: Consider containerizing your Java applications using Docker for consistent and reproducible builds and deployments.

- **Monitor CI/CD Pipelines**: Regularly monitor your CI/CD pipelines to identify and address issues promptly.

- **Security Scanning**: Integrate security scanning tools into your CI pipeline to identify vulnerabilities in your code and dependencies.

- **Documentation**: Maintain documentation for your CI/CD processes and workflows to facilitate onboarding and troubleshooting.

By implementing CI in your Java development workflow, you can ensure that your codebase remains stable, reliable, and continuously improved. It helps catch bugs early, streamline development processes, and deliver high-quality software to users.

Chapter 7: Database Programming with JDBC

7.1 Connecting to Databases

In this section, we'll delve into the world of database programming with Java using JDBC (Java Database Connectivity). JDBC is a Java-based API that allows Java applications to interact with relational databases. We'll explore how to connect to databases, manage database connections, and perform basic database operations.

JDBC Overview

JDBC provides a standardized way to connect to databases, execute SQL queries, and manipulate database data from Java applications. It serves as a bridge between the Java programming language and various relational databases like MySQL, PostgreSQL, Oracle, and more.

Connecting to a Database

To connect to a database using JDBC, you need the following information:

- **JDBC URL**: A URL that specifies the database's location and access protocol.

- **Database Driver**: A JDBC driver that corresponds to the database you're using. Each database typically has its own JDBC driver.

- **Database Credentials**: Username and password with the necessary privileges to access the database.

JDBC drivers are platform-specific implementations that enable Java applications to communicate with particular databases. There are four types of JDBC drivers:

1. **Type 1: JDBC-ODBC Bridge Driver**: This driver uses ODBC (Open Database Connectivity) to connect to databases. It's suitable for databases that support ODBC.

2. **Type 2: Native-API Driver**: This driver calls the database's native API to interact with the database. It requires a native library specific to the database system.

3. **Type 3: Network Protocol Driver**: This driver translates JDBC calls into a database-independent network protocol, which is then translated into database-specific calls on the server.

4. **Type 4: Thin Driver**: Also known as the Direct-to-Database Pure Java Driver, this driver communicates directly with the database server. It's platform-independent and doesn't require native code.

Establishing a Database Connection

To establish a connection to a database, you need to load the JDBC driver, create a connection URL, and use the DriverManager class to create a connection instance. Here's a basic example:

```java
import java.sql.Connection;
import java.sql.DriverManager;
import java.sql.SQLException;

public class DatabaseConnector {
    public static void main(String[] args) {
        // JDBC URL, username, and password
        String jdbcUrl = "jdbc:mysql://localhost:3306/mydb";
        String username = "user";
        String password = "password";

        try {
            // Load the JDBC driver
            Class.forName("com.mysql.cj.jdbc.Driver");

            // Establish a connection
            Connection connection = DriverManager.getConnection(jdbcUrl, username, password);

            // Do database operations here

            // Close the connection when done
```

```
            connection.close();
        } catch (ClassNotFoundException | SQLException e) {
            e.printStackTrace();
        }
    }
}
```

Closing the Connection

It's essential to close the database connection when you're done to release resources and avoid memory leaks. You can use the `close()` method on the `Connection` object:

```
connection.close();
```

Conclusion

In this section, we've introduced the fundamentals of database programming with JDBC in Java. We discussed the importance of JDBC, JDBC drivers, and the process of establishing a database connection. In the upcoming sections, we'll explore executing SQL queries, handling result sets, and more advanced JDBC topics.

Chapter 11: Java Security

11.1 Common Security Vulnerabilities

In this section, we'll dive into the realm of security in Java applications. Security is a critical aspect of software development, and understanding common security vulnerabilities is essential for building robust and secure Java applications.

Importance of Security

Security is a top concern in today's digital landscape. Malicious actors constantly seek vulnerabilities in software to exploit, potentially leading to data breaches, financial losses, and reputational damage. Java applications, like any other software, are susceptible to security vulnerabilities, making it crucial for developers to be aware of these issues.

Common Security Vulnerabilities

Let's explore some of the common security vulnerabilities that Java developers should be vigilant about:

1. **Injection Attacks**: Injection attacks occur when untrusted data is sent to an interpreter as part of a query or command. Common examples include SQL injection, where attackers manipulate database queries, and XML injection, which targets XML parsers.

2. **Cross-Site Scripting (XSS)**: XSS vulnerabilities allow attackers to inject malicious scripts into web pages viewed by other users. This can lead to session hijacking, data theft, and other security breaches.

3. **Cross-Site Request Forgery (CSRF)**: CSRF attacks trick users into performing actions on websites without their consent. Attackers exploit the trust that a user has in a particular website.

4. **Broken Authentication**: Weak authentication mechanisms or improper session management can lead to unauthorized access to sensitive areas of an application.

5. **Insecure Deserialization**: When an application deserializes data from an untrusted source, it can lead to code execution attacks. Deserialization vulnerabilities are often challenging to detect and mitigate.

6. **Security Misconfigurations**: Poorly configured security settings, unnecessary services, and excessive permissions can create openings for attackers.

7. **Sensitive Data Exposure**: Failure to properly protect sensitive data, such as passwords and financial information, can result in data breaches and privacy violations.

8. **Insecure Dependencies**: Java applications often rely on third-party libraries. If these libraries have known vulnerabilities or are not kept up to date, they can become entry points for attackers.

9. **Using Deprecated or Weak Algorithms**: Cryptographic vulnerabilities can arise from the use of deprecated or weak algorithms for encryption and hashing.

10. **Insufficient Logging and Monitoring**: Inadequate logging and monitoring make it challenging to detect and respond to security incidents in a timely manner.

Mitigating Security Vulnerabilities

To address these vulnerabilities, developers must follow secure coding practices, use security libraries and frameworks, conduct regular security assessments, and stay informed about the latest security threats and patches. The Java ecosystem offers various security tools and best practices to help mitigate security risks.

In the subsequent sections of this chapter, we'll delve deeper into securing Java applications, including authentication and authorization, cryptography, and best practices for Java security. Building secure software is an ongoing process, and developers must prioritize security at every stage of application development.

11.2 Securing Java Applications

Securing Java applications is of paramount importance to protect sensitive data, user privacy, and the overall integrity of your software. In this section, we'll explore various aspects of securing Java applications and the best practices that can be followed.

Authentication and Authorization

Authentication is the process of verifying the identity of users, ensuring they are who they claim to be. Authorization, on the other hand, determines what actions authenticated users are allowed to perform within the application.

Authentication

In Java, authentication can be implemented using various methods:

- **Username and Password**: This is the most common form of authentication, where users provide their username and password to access the application. Java provides libraries and frameworks like Spring Security to implement this.

- **Token-Based Authentication**: Token-based authentication involves issuing tokens to users upon successful login. These tokens are then sent with each subsequent request to authenticate the user. Libraries like JSON Web Tokens (JWT) are often used for this purpose.

Authorization

Authorization defines what actions or resources a user is allowed to access based on their role or permissions. Role-based access control (RBAC) and attribute-based access control (ABAC) are common authorization models.

In Java, authorization can be implemented using frameworks and libraries that provide role-based or permission-based access control. Spring Security, for instance, allows developers to define access rules based on roles.

Input Validation

Proper input validation is crucial to prevent various types of attacks, such as SQL injection and cross-site scripting (XSS). Always validate and sanitize user inputs before processing them. Java provides validation libraries like Hibernate Validator and Apache Commons Validator that can assist in this regard.

Data Encryption

To protect sensitive data, encryption is essential. Java offers libraries for encryption and decryption, such as the Java Cryptography Architecture (JCA) and the Java Cryptography Extension (JCE). Use strong encryption algorithms and secure key management practices.

Secure Coding Practices

Follow secure coding practices to avoid common pitfalls. Some essential practices include:

- Avoiding hardcoding sensitive information like passwords and API keys in source code.
- Regularly updating dependencies to patch known vulnerabilities.
- Implementing proper error handling and not revealing sensitive information in error messages.
- Sanitizing user inputs and avoiding the use of raw SQL queries.

Logging and Monitoring

Implement robust logging and monitoring to detect and respond to security incidents. Logging should capture relevant security-related events, and monitoring should include intrusion detection and alerting mechanisms.

Security Testing

Conduct regular security testing, including penetration testing and code reviews, to identify vulnerabilities early in the development process. Automated security scanning tools can also help uncover potential issues.

Patch Management

Stay up to date with security patches and updates for your application's components, including the Java runtime, libraries, and the operating system. Timely patching can prevent known vulnerabilities from being exploited.

Education and Training

Finally, ensure that your development team is well-educated about security best practices. Offer training and resources to keep everyone informed about emerging threats and mitigation strategies.

By following these security practices, you can significantly enhance the security posture of your Java applications and reduce the risk of security breaches and data compromises. Remember that security is an ongoing process and should be integrated into every phase of your application's lifecycle.

11.3 Authentication and Authorization

Authentication and authorization are critical aspects of securing Java applications, ensuring that only authorized users can access certain resources and perform specific actions. In this section, we'll delve deeper into these concepts.

Authentication

Authentication verifies the identity of a user or system. It ensures that users are who they claim to be before granting access to an application or its resources.

Common Authentication Methods

1. **Username and Password**: This is the most common method where users provide a username and password during login. Java provides built-in support for username and password-based authentication.

```java
// Example of authenticating a user with username and password
public boolean authenticate(String username, String password) {
    // Validate username and password against a database or user store
    // Return true if the credentials are valid, false otherwise
}
```

2. **Token-Based Authentication**: Tokens, such as JSON Web Tokens (JWT), are used to authenticate users. A token is issued upon successful login and must be sent with each request for authorization.

```java
// Example of JWT authentication
String token = generateToken(username, roles);
// Include the token in the request header for subsequent requests
```

3. **OAuth 2.0**: OAuth 2.0 is a widely-used protocol for delegated authorization. It allows applications to obtain limited access to user resources without exposing credentials.

Multi-Factor Authentication (MFA)

Multi-factor authentication adds an extra layer of security by requiring users to provide multiple forms of verification. Common factors include something the user knows (password), something the user has (a smartphone or hardware token), and something the user is (biometrics like fingerprint or facial recognition).

Authorization

Authorization determines what actions or resources a user can access after successful authentication. It enforces access control based on roles, permissions, or policies.

Role-Based Access Control (RBAC)

RBAC is a widely-used authorization model where users are assigned roles, and roles have specific permissions. Users inherit the permissions associated with their roles.

```
// Example of RBAC in Spring Security
@PreAuthorize("hasRole('ADMIN')")
public void deleteResource() {
    // Delete a resource, but only if the user has the 'ADMIN' role
}
```

Attribute-Based Access Control (ABAC)

ABAC is a more flexible authorization model that considers various attributes when making access control decisions. Attributes can include user attributes, resource attributes, and environmental attributes.

```
// Example of ABAC using Spring Security's SpEL expressions
@PreAuthorize("#resource.owner == principal.username")
public void editResource(Resource resource) {
    // Allow editing the resource only if the user is the owner
}
```

Best Practices for Authentication and Authorization

1. **Use Strong Authentication Methods**: Choose authentication methods that fit your application's security needs. Stronger methods like MFA should be considered for sensitive applications.

2. **Implement Principle of Least Privilege (PoLP)**: Assign the minimum level of access necessary for each user or system. Avoid over-privileging users.

3. **Regularly Review and Update Access Controls**: Periodically review and update roles, permissions, and access control policies to adapt to changing requirements.

4. **Protect User Credentials**: Store user passwords securely using strong hashing algorithms, and never store them in plaintext. Use password salting for added security.

5. **Audit and Monitor**: Implement robust auditing and monitoring of authentication and authorization events to detect suspicious activities.

6. **Secure Communication**: Use secure communication protocols (e.g., HTTPS) to protect data in transit during authentication and authorization processes.

7. **Error Handling**: Ensure that error messages do not reveal sensitive information about authentication or authorization failures.

8. **Regular Security Testing**: Perform security testing, including penetration testing and code reviews, to identify vulnerabilities and weaknesses.

By implementing sound authentication and authorization practices, you can bolster the security of your Java applications and safeguard sensitive data from unauthorized access. Remember that security is an ongoing process, and it's crucial to stay informed about emerging threats and best practices in the field of authentication and authorization.

11.4 Cryptography in Java

Cryptography plays a fundamental role in securing sensitive data and communications within Java applications. Java provides a robust set of cryptographic tools and libraries to facilitate encryption, decryption, hashing, and digital signatures. In this section, we'll explore the key aspects of cryptography in Java.

Key Concepts

Encryption and Decryption

Encryption is the process of converting plaintext data into ciphertext to protect it from unauthorized access. Decryption is the reverse process, converting ciphertext back to plaintext.

Java provides various encryption algorithms, such as Advanced Encryption Standard (AES), RSA, and Triple Data Encryption Standard (3DES), through its `javax.crypto` package.

```java
// Example of AES encryption and decryption
Cipher cipher = Cipher.getInstance("AES/CBC/PKCS5Padding");
SecretKeySpec secretKey = new SecretKeySpec(key, "AES");
cipher.init(Cipher.ENCRYPT_MODE, secretKey);
byte[] encryptedData = cipher.doFinal(plainText);

cipher.init(Cipher.DECRYPT_MODE, secretKey);
byte[] decryptedData = cipher.doFinal(encryptedData);
```

Hashing

Hashing is a one-way function that transforms data into a fixed-length hash value. It is commonly used to store passwords securely and verify data integrity.

Java provides hashing algorithms like SHA-256 and MD5 through the `java.security.MessageDigest` class.

```java
// Example of SHA-256 hashing
MessageDigest digest = MessageDigest.getInstance("SHA-256");
byte[] hashedBytes = digest.digest(plainText.getBytes(StandardCharsets.UTF_8)
);
```

Digital Signatures

Digital signatures are used to verify the authenticity and integrity of digital messages or documents. Java supports digital signatures through the `java.security.Signature` class.

```java
// Example of creating and verifying digital signatures
Signature signature = Signature.getInstance("SHA256withRSA");
signature.initSign(privateKey);
signature.update(dataToSign);
byte[] digitalSignature = signature.sign();

signature.initVerify(publicKey);
signature.update(dataToSign);
boolean verified = signature.verify(digitalSignature);
```

Java Cryptography Architecture (JCA) and Java Cryptography Extension (JCE)

The Java Cryptography Architecture (JCA) and Java Cryptography Extension (JCE) provide a framework for implementing cryptographic functionality in Java applications. JCA defines the architecture and APIs, while JCE extends it with cryptographic service providers (CSPs).

Java ships with a default CSP, but you can install and use additional CSPs to support different algorithms and security mechanisms.

SecureRandom

SecureRandom is a class that provides cryptographically strong random number generation. It's essential for generating secure cryptographic keys and initialization vectors.

```java
// Example of generating a secure random key
SecureRandom secureRandom = SecureRandom.getInstanceStrong();
byte[] randomKey = new byte[16];
secureRandom.nextBytes(randomKey);
```

Best Practices for Cryptography in Java

1. **Use Strong Algorithms**: Choose cryptographic algorithms that are considered secure and avoid deprecated or weak algorithms.

2. **Key Management**: Protect cryptographic keys and never hardcode them in your source code. Use a secure key management system.

3. **Initialization Vectors (IVs)**: When using block ciphers like AES in modes that require IVs, ensure that IVs are unique for each encryption operation.

4. **Salting for Hashing**: When hashing passwords, use a unique salt for each user to prevent rainbow table attacks.

5. **Regular Updates**: Keep your Java environment up-to-date with the latest security patches and updates.

6. **Security Audits**: Periodically conduct security audits and penetration testing to identify vulnerabilities in your cryptographic implementations.

7. **Secure Key Storage**: Store cryptographic keys securely using hardware security modules (HSMs) or key management services.

By following best practices and using the cryptographic tools provided by Java, you can enhance the security of your applications and protect sensitive data and communications from unauthorized access and tampering. Remember that cryptographic security is a complex field, so seek expert guidance when dealing with sensitive information.

11.5 Best Practices for Java Security

Security is a critical aspect of software development, and Java provides several mechanisms and best practices to help developers create secure applications. In this section, we'll explore some key best practices for enhancing the security of Java applications.

1. Input Validation

Always validate and sanitize user input to prevent common security vulnerabilities like SQL injection and cross-site scripting (XSS). Use libraries like OWASP's Java Encoder to sanitize data.

```
String sanitizedInput = Encoder.forHtml(contentFromUser);
```

2. Authentication and Authorization

Implement strong authentication mechanisms to ensure that users are who they claim to be. Java provides libraries like Spring Security for comprehensive authentication and authorization.

```java
// Spring Security configuration for authentication
@Override
protected void configure(AuthenticationManagerBuilder auth) throws Exception
{
    auth
        .inMemoryAuthentication()
        .withUser("user")
        .password(passwordEncoder().encode("password"))
        .roles("
```

Chapter 12: JavaFX for Mobile and Embedded Systems

JavaFX, originally designed for desktop applications, has evolved to cater to mobile and embedded systems. In this chapter, we will explore the adaptation of JavaFX for various mobile devices and embedded platforms, including smartphones, tablets, embedded systems, and the Internet of Things (IoT).

12.1 JavaFX on Mobile Devices

JavaFX allows developers to build cross-platform mobile applications using the same codebase, making it a versatile choice for mobile app development. The key to achieving this is the use of JavaFXPorts, which is an open-source project aimed at bringing JavaFX to mobile platforms.

JavaFXPorts provides a plugin for Gradle or Maven that simplifies the build and deployment process for Android and iOS. Developers can create mobile applications using JavaFX, and then with minimal platform-specific adjustments, deploy them to both Android and iOS devices.

To get started with JavaFX on mobile devices, follow these general steps:

1. **Install JavaFXPorts**: You can download the JavaFXPorts SDK and install it on your development machine.

2. **Set Up Your Development Environment**: Configure your development environment for both Android and iOS development. This may include setting up Android Studio for Android development and Xcode for iOS development.

3. **Create Your JavaFX Application**: Write your JavaFX mobile application as you would for a desktop application. Ensure that it adheres to mobile design guidelines for a better user experience.

4. **Configure Your Build**: Use the JavaFXPorts Gradle or Maven plugin to configure your project for Android and iOS. Specify the target platforms, icons, and other platform-specific settings.

5. **Build and Deploy**: Use Gradle or Maven commands to build your application for Android and iOS. Deploy the generated APK (for Android) and IPA (for iOS) files to the respective app stores or devices.

6. **Testing**: Test your application on various Android and iOS devices to ensure it works as expected.

By following these steps, you can leverage JavaFX to develop mobile applications for Android and iOS efficiently. JavaFX's capabilities for creating rich user interfaces and the ability to share code between platforms make it a compelling choice for mobile development.

In the following sections, we will delve into using JavaFX for embedded systems and explore how it can be applied to various IoT scenarios.

12.2 Building JavaFX Applications for Embedded Systems

JavaFX's adaptability extends beyond mobile devices to embedded systems, where it can power user interfaces for various applications, including kiosks, point-of-sale (POS) terminals, industrial control systems, and more. Building JavaFX applications for embedded systems involves considerations such as hardware constraints, custom touch interfaces, and deployment options.

Hardware and Resource Constraints

When developing for embedded systems, it's crucial to be aware of the hardware limitations of the target device. These limitations can include limited processing power, memory, and screen size. JavaFX allows developers to create lightweight and efficient user interfaces to accommodate these constraints.

Here are some strategies for building JavaFX applications for embedded systems:

1. **Optimize Resource Usage**: Minimize the memory footprint of your application by reducing unnecessary object creation and memory consumption. Use JavaFX's built-in memory management features to help manage memory efficiently.

2. **Custom UI Design**: Design your user interface to fit the specific screen size and input methods of the embedded device. JavaFX's flexible layout management allows you to create custom UIs tailored to your needs.

3. **Touch and Gesture Support**: Many embedded systems use touch screens. JavaFX provides robust support for touch and gesture interactions, making it suitable for touch-based embedded applications.

Deployment Options

Deploying JavaFX applications on embedded systems can vary depending on the target platform. Some common deployment options include:

1. **Standalone Deployment**: In this scenario, the JavaFX application runs directly on the embedded hardware without the need for a web browser. You can bundle the Java Runtime Environment (JRE) with your application for a self-contained deployment.

2. **Web Start**: Java Web Start allows users to launch JavaFX applications from a web browser. While less common for embedded systems, it can be a suitable option for certain use cases.

3. **Java Packager**: The Java Packager tool enables you to package your JavaFX application as an executable binary for specific platforms, including Linux,

Windows, and macOS. You can customize the packaging process to meet the requirements of your embedded system.

4. **Embedded Operating Systems**: Some embedded systems run on custom operating systems. In such cases, you may need to adapt your JavaFX application to run within the constraints of the operating system.

Real-World Applications

JavaFX's adaptability to embedded systems has been demonstrated in real-world applications. For example, it has been used to create user interfaces for medical devices, industrial control panels, and automotive infotainment systems. These applications benefit from JavaFX's rich graphics capabilities and flexibility in designing custom UIs.

When building JavaFX applications for embedded systems, collaboration with embedded hardware and software experts is essential to ensure that the application meets the performance and reliability requirements of the target device. JavaFX's versatility and robustness make it a viable choice for a wide range of embedded system applications.

12.3 Java ME (Micro Edition)

Java ME, short for Java Micro Edition, is a platform that extends the capabilities of Java to resource-constrained devices, especially those with limited memory, processing power, and display capabilities. It's designed for embedded systems, feature phones, and other devices where the full Java SE platform may not be practical.

Key Features of Java ME

Java ME offers several key features that make it suitable for developing applications on resource-constrained devices:

1. **Small Footprint**: Java ME has a compact runtime environment that consumes minimal memory and storage space, making it ideal for devices with limited resources.

2. **Platform Independence**: Like Java SE, Java ME applications are platform-independent, allowing developers to write code once and run it on various Java ME-enabled devices.

3. **APIs for Embedded Systems**: Java ME includes APIs tailored for embedded systems, such as sensor access, low-level hardware control, and user interface design for small screens.

4. **Security**: It provides security features for applications running on devices, including user authentication and data encryption.

5. **Connectivity**: Java ME supports various communication protocols, including HTTP, Bluetooth, and SMS, enabling devices to connect to networks and communicate with other devices.

Developing Java ME applications involves using the Java ME Software Development Kit (SDK) and the Java ME Development Environment (JDE). Here's a high-level overview of the development process:

1. **Install the Java ME SDK**: Download and install the Java ME SDK, which includes tools, emulators, and libraries for developing Java ME applications.

2. **Create a Java ME Project**: Use the SDK to create a new Java ME project. You can specify the target device and configuration for your application.

3. **Write Java ME Code**: Write the application code using the Java ME APIs and libraries. These APIs are optimized for small devices and provide functionality for user interfaces, networking, and device-specific features.

4. **Test Using Emulators**: Java ME SDK provides emulators that simulate the behavior of various Java ME-enabled devices. You can test and debug your application using these emulators.

5. **Package and Deploy**: Once your application is ready, you can package it into a format suitable for deployment on the target device. The packaging format may vary depending on the device and configuration.

Java ME has been used in a wide range of applications, including:

- **Mobile Phones**: Java ME was commonly used for developing games, utilities, and applications for feature phones before the rise of smartphones.

- **IoT Devices**: It's used in IoT devices for sensor data collection, remote monitoring, and control.

- **Smart Cards**: Java Card, a subset of Java ME, is used in smart cards for secure transactions and authentication.

- **Industrial Automation**: Java ME is employed in industrial automation systems and programmable logic controllers (PLCs) for process control and monitoring.

- **Telematics**: It's used in vehicle tracking and fleet management systems.

- **Point-of-Sale Terminals**: Java ME powers point-of-sale terminals in retail environments.

Java ME continues to find applications in scenarios where resource-constrained devices require a robust and platform-independent development platform. Its ability to run on a wide range of devices makes it a valuable tool for embedded systems development.

12.4 Internet of Things (IoT) with Java

The Internet of Things (IoT) represents a network of interconnected devices and sensors that collect and exchange data over the internet. Java plays a significant role in IoT development due to its platform independence, security features, and the availability of libraries and frameworks tailored for IoT applications.

Benefits of Using Java for IoT

Java offers several advantages for IoT development:

1. **Platform Independence**: Java applications can run on various hardware platforms and operating systems, making it easier to develop IoT solutions that work across different devices.

2. **Security**: IoT devices often handle sensitive data, and Java provides robust security mechanisms, including authentication, encryption, and access control.

3. **Large Developer Community**: Java has a vast developer community, which means readily available resources, libraries, and tools for IoT projects.

4. **Scalability**: IoT applications can range from small-scale deployments to large-scale solutions. Java's scalability allows developers to adapt to different project sizes.

5. **Remote Device Management**: Java supports remote device management, enabling administrators to update and monitor IoT devices remotely.

Developing IoT Applications with Java

Developing IoT applications with Java involves the following steps:

1. **Select the Hardware**: Choose the appropriate IoT hardware for your project, such as sensors, microcontrollers, and communication modules. Ensure that the hardware supports Java or has a Java Virtual Machine (JVM) available.

2. **Setup Development Environment**: Install the necessary tools for IoT development, including the Java Development Kit (JDK) and any IoT-specific libraries or frameworks you plan to use.

3. **Write IoT Code**: Develop the application code using Java. You'll need to interface with sensors, handle data processing, and establish communication with other devices or a central server.

4. **Implement Connectivity**: IoT devices need to communicate with each other or with cloud services. Java provides libraries for handling various communication protocols, including MQTT, CoAP, and HTTP.

5. **Security Considerations**: Implement security measures to protect data and device integrity. This includes secure data transmission, device authentication, and access control.

6. **Testing and Deployment**: Thoroughly test your IoT application in a controlled environment before deploying it to the target devices. Consider using simulators or emulators for testing.

7. **Device Management**: Implement remote device management capabilities, allowing you to update firmware, configure devices, and monitor their status remotely.

Java Libraries and Frameworks for IoT

Several Java libraries and frameworks simplify IoT development:

1. **Eclipse IoT**: Eclipse IoT provides a set of open-source projects for building IoT solutions. It includes libraries for device communication, protocols, and cloud connectivity.

2. **Java ME (Micro Edition)**: As mentioned earlier, Java ME is suitable for resource-constrained IoT devices, especially those with limited memory and processing power.

3. **Eclipse Kura**: An open-source framework for building IoT gateways, Kura offers Java APIs for developing IoT applications that run on gateways.

4. **Azure IoT SDK for Java**: Microsoft's Azure IoT SDK includes Java libraries for connecting devices to the Azure IoT Hub, enabling seamless integration with Azure cloud services.

5. **AWS IoT SDK for Java**: Amazon Web Services (AWS) offers a Java SDK for IoT, allowing devices to connect to AWS IoT Core for data processing and management.

Real-World IoT Applications with Java

Java is widely used in various IoT applications:

- **Smart Homes**: Java is used to develop applications that control smart home devices, such as thermostats, lights, and security systems.

- **Industrial IoT (IIoT)**: In manufacturing and industrial settings, Java is employed to monitor and control machinery, collect sensor data, and optimize production processes.

- **Agriculture**: IoT sensors and Java applications help farmers monitor soil conditions, weather, and crop health to improve agricultural yields.

- **Healthcare**: IoT devices and Java applications assist in remote patient monitoring, wearable health devices, and hospital equipment management.

- **Smart Cities**: Java is used in smart city projects to manage traffic, street lighting, waste management, and environmental monitoring.

Java's versatility and extensive ecosystem make it a valuable tool for developing IoT solutions, enabling developers to create innovative applications that connect and interact with the physical world.

12.5 Challenges and Opportunities

As we delve into the final section of this book, it's essential to explore the challenges and opportunities that lie ahead in the world of Java and emerging technologies. Java has continuously evolved to meet the demands of modern software development, and it will continue to play a crucial role in the technology landscape. However, this evolving landscape also presents new challenges and opportunities.

Challenges

1. **Keeping Up with Language Evolution**: Java continues to evolve with new language features and updates. Developers need to stay current with the latest developments to write efficient and maintainable code.

2. **Security Concerns**: With the increasing sophistication of cyberattacks, security remains a significant concern. Java developers must prioritize secure coding practices and stay updated on security best practices.

3. **Performance Optimization**: As applications become more complex, optimizing performance becomes crucial. Developers must profile and tune their applications to ensure they meet performance requirements.

4. **Cross-Platform Compatibility**: While Java's "write once, run anywhere" mantra remains, ensuring cross-platform compatibility across different devices and environments can be challenging.

5. **Concurrency and Multithreading**: Building concurrent and multithreaded applications correctly is challenging but essential for taking full advantage of modern hardware.

6. **Adoption of New Technologies**: Keeping up with new technologies and integrating them into existing systems is a continuous challenge. This includes adopting technologies like containers, microservices, and cloud-native architectures.

Opportunities

1. **Quantum Computing**: Java is likely to play a role in the emerging field of quantum computing as it becomes more practical. Developers can explore quantum libraries and tools to prepare for this exciting future.

2. **Blockchain and Cryptocurrency**: As blockchain and cryptocurrency technologies gain traction, Java developers have opportunities to work on decentralized applications and smart contracts.

3. **Artificial Intelligence and Machine Learning**: Java is used in various AI and ML libraries and frameworks. Developers can explore these fields to build intelligent applications.

4. **Augmented and Virtual Reality**: Java is relevant in AR and VR development, creating immersive experiences in gaming, education, and training.

5. **IoT and Edge Computing**: IoT and edge computing are growing rapidly. Java developers can build applications for smart devices and edge servers.

6. **Cloud-Native Development**: With the shift towards cloud-native architectures, Java developers can explore containerization, orchestration, and microservices to build scalable and resilient applications.

7. **Open Source Contributions**: Contributing to open source projects is a valuable opportunity for developers to gain experience and recognition in the community.

8. **Education and Training**: With the demand for skilled Java developers, opportunities exist for educators and trainers to provide learning resources and courses.

9. **Consulting and Freelancing**: Experienced Java developers can offer consulting and freelance services to organizations looking to modernize their Java applications.

10. **Startup Ventures**: Entrepreneurial developers can explore startup opportunities, creating innovative products and services based on Java and emerging technologies.

In conclusion, Java's journey continues in the rapidly evolving world of technology. While challenges exist, the opportunities for Java developers are abundant. Staying curious, adaptable, and committed to learning will be key to thriving in this dynamic landscape. Java's principles of platform independence, security, and community-driven development remain as relevant as ever, ensuring its enduring significance in the years to come.

Chapter 13: Java for Big Data

13.1 Introduction to Big Data

In today's digital age, data has become an invaluable resource. The amount of data generated daily is staggering, and traditional data processing methods often fall short when dealing with such large volumes of information. This is where Big Data technologies come into play, and Java has a significant role to play in this space.

What is Big Data?

Big Data refers to extremely large and complex datasets that cannot be effectively managed, processed, or analyzed using traditional data processing tools. These datasets typically include a variety of data types, such as structured, semi-structured, and unstructured data. The three primary characteristics of Big Data are often referred to as the "3Vs":

1. **Volume**: Big Data involves vast amounts of data. It can range from terabytes to petabytes and beyond.

2. **Velocity**: Data is generated at an unprecedented speed, often in real-time or near real-time. Examples include social media posts, sensor data, and financial transactions.

3. **Variety**: Big Data encompasses diverse data types, including text, images, videos, and more. This data may come from different sources and in various formats.

The Importance of Big Data

Big Data analytics has revolutionized various industries by providing valuable insights and enabling data-driven decision-making. Here are some key areas where Big Data has made a significant impact:

- **Business Intelligence**: Companies use Big Data analytics to gain insights into customer behavior, market trends, and competitive intelligence.

- **Healthcare**: Big Data helps healthcare professionals improve patient care, diagnose diseases, and streamline healthcare operations.

- **Finance**: Financial institutions use Big Data to detect fraud, manage risk, and make investment decisions.

- **Manufacturing**: Manufacturers leverage Big Data to optimize production processes, reduce downtime, and enhance product quality.

- **E-commerce**: Online retailers use Big Data to personalize recommendations, optimize pricing, and manage inventory.

- **Social Media**: Social media platforms analyze Big Data to enhance user experiences, deliver targeted advertising, and detect trends.

- **Scientific Research**: Big Data is used in scientific research, including genomics, climate modeling, and particle physics.

Java has established itself as a prominent language in the Big Data ecosystem. Its characteristics, including platform independence, scalability, and a vast ecosystem of libraries and frameworks, make it a suitable choice for Big Data development. Here's how Java is used in the world of Big Data:

- **Hadoop**: Java is the primary language for developing applications in the Hadoop ecosystem. Hadoop is an open-source framework for distributed storage and processing of Big Data. Developers use Java to write MapReduce programs for data processing.

- **Apache Spark**: Apache Spark, a fast and general-purpose cluster computing framework, provides Java APIs for building Big Data applications. It's known for its in-memory processing capabilities.

- **Apache Flink**: Flink is another stream processing framework that offers Java APIs for real-time data processing. It's used in applications like event-driven systems and IoT.

- **Data Serialization**: Java provides efficient data serialization mechanisms like Avro and Protocol Buffers, which are essential for data storage and interchange in Big Data systems.

- **Integration**: Java integrates with various Big Data technologies and databases, making it a versatile language for building end-to-end Big Data solutions.

In the following sections of this chapter, we will explore specific Big Data technologies and how Java is used in each of them. Whether you're a data engineer, data scientist, or software developer, understanding Java's role in Big Data can open up exciting opportunities in this field.

13.2 Hadoop and MapReduce

In the world of Big Data, Hadoop and MapReduce are household names. Hadoop is an open-source framework that allows distributed storage and processing of large datasets, and MapReduce is a programming model and processing engine used within the Hadoop framework. Let's dive into what Hadoop and MapReduce are all about and how Java plays a significant role in this ecosystem.

Hadoop, developed by the Apache Software Foundation, is an open-source framework designed to store and process large datasets in a distributed computing environment. The core components of Hadoop include:

- **Hadoop Distributed File System (HDFS)**: HDFS is a distributed file system designed to store vast amounts of data across multiple machines. It divides data into blocks and replicates them across the cluster for fault tolerance.

- **MapReduce**: MapReduce is a programming model for processing and generating large datasets that parallelizes the computation across a distributed cluster. It consists of two main phases: the Map phase and the Reduce phase.

- **YARN (Yet Another Resource Negotiator)**: YARN is the resource management layer of Hadoop. It manages resources and schedules applications for efficient cluster utilization.

How MapReduce Works

MapReduce is a powerful and flexible data processing model for distributed computing. It breaks down data processing into two phases:

1. **Map Phase**: In this phase, data is divided into chunks, and each chunk is processed independently by a Mapper function. The Mapper function takes an input key-value pair and produces intermediate key-value pairs as output.

2. **Shuffle and Sort**: The intermediate key-value pairs generated by the Mappers are grouped and sorted by key. This step ensures that all values for a particular key are processed together in the next phase.

3. **Reduce Phase**: In the Reduce phase, the sorted intermediate key-value pairs are processed by the Reducer function. The Reducer function takes a key and the associated list of values and produces the final output.

Java and Hadoop

Java is the primary language used for developing applications in the Hadoop ecosystem. Hadoop provides Java APIs for writing MapReduce programs, making it accessible to Java developers. Here's how Java fits into the Hadoop workflow:

1. **Writing MapReduce Jobs**: Java developers write MapReduce jobs in Java, defining the Mapper and Reducer functions. These jobs are then submitted to the Hadoop cluster for execution.

2. **Hadoop Streaming**: Hadoop also supports other languages through Hadoop Streaming, but Java remains the most common choice. Hadoop Streaming allows developers to use any programming language that can read from standard input and write to standard output to interact with the Hadoop MapReduce framework.

3. **Hadoop Libraries**: Java libraries and frameworks like Apache HBase, Apache Pig, and Apache Hive are built on top of Hadoop, providing higher-level abstractions for data processing.

4. **Integration**: Java applications can easily integrate with Hadoop clusters to perform tasks such as data ingestion, data processing, and result retrieval.

In summary, Java is an integral part of the Hadoop ecosystem, enabling developers to harness the power of distributed computing for processing Big Data. Java's familiarity, performance, and extensive libraries make it a preferred choice for building Hadoop applications. Whether you're dealing with massive log files, analyzing customer behavior, or processing sensor data, Hadoop and Java together provide the tools to tackle the challenges of Big Data.

13.3 Apache Spark

Apache Spark is a powerful open-source data processing engine designed for big data processing and analytics. It has gained immense popularity in the field of data engineering and data science due to its speed, ease of use, and versatility. In this section, we'll explore what Apache Spark is, how it differs from Hadoop MapReduce, and how Java fits into the Spark ecosystem.

What is Apache Spark?

Apache Spark is a cluster computing framework that provides in-memory data processing capabilities. It was developed to address the limitations of the Hadoop MapReduce model, which relies heavily on disk storage, making it slow for iterative algorithms and interactive data analysis.

Key features of Apache Spark include:

- **In-Memory Processing**: Spark caches data in memory, reducing the need to read from disk repeatedly, which significantly improves processing speed.

- **Versatility**: Spark supports various data processing workloads, including batch processing, interactive queries, machine learning, and stream processing, all within a unified framework.

- **Ease of Use**: Spark provides high-level APIs in multiple languages, including Java, Scala, Python, and R, making it accessible to a wide range of developers.

- **Resilient Distributed Datasets (RDDs)**: RDDs are Spark's fundamental data abstraction, offering fault tolerance and distributed data processing capabilities.

Apache Spark works by breaking down data processing tasks into smaller, parallelizable units. Here's a simplified overview of how Spark processes data:

1. **Data Ingestion**: Data is ingested into Spark from various sources, such as HDFS, Apache Kafka, or external databases.

2. **Transformation**: Spark allows developers to apply transformations to the data using high-level operations like `map`, `filter`, and `reduce`. These transformations create a directed acyclic graph (DAG) of tasks.

3. **Action**: Actions are operations that trigger the execution of the DAG. Examples of actions include `collect`, `count`, and `saveAsTextFile`. When an action is executed, Spark calculates the result by performing the necessary transformations in parallel across the cluster.

4. **In-Memory Processing**: Spark caches intermediate data in memory, minimizing the need for redundant reads from disk. This in-memory processing is one of the reasons for Spark's speed.

Java and Apache Spark

Java is one of the primary languages supported by Apache Spark, alongside Scala, Python, and R. Java developers can leverage Spark's capabilities using the Spark Java API. Here's how Java is used in Apache Spark:

1. **Spark Java API**: Developers can write Spark applications in Java using the Spark Java API. This API provides classes and methods for creating Spark jobs, defining transformations, and executing actions.

2. **Integration with Hadoop**: Spark can run on Hadoop clusters, allowing Java applications to integrate with existing Hadoop-based workflows. Spark can read data from HDFS and interact with other Hadoop ecosystem components.

3. **Performance**: Java applications running on Spark benefit from its in-memory processing capabilities, making them significantly faster than equivalent Hadoop MapReduce jobs.

4. **Ecosystem Integration**: Apache Spark has a rich ecosystem of libraries and extensions, including MLlib for machine learning and Spark Streaming for real-time data processing. Java developers can utilize these libraries to build sophisticated data pipelines and analytical applications.

In conclusion, Apache Spark is a versatile and high-performance data processing engine that offers Java developers a powerful platform for tackling big data analytics and processing tasks. Java's strong integration with Spark, coupled with Spark's speed and ease of use, makes it a compelling choice for data engineers and data scientists working with large datasets.

13.4 Processing Big Data with Java

Java is a versatile and widely-used programming language that plays a crucial role in processing big data. In this section, we'll explore how Java is used for processing and analyzing large datasets, often referred to as "big data."

Big Data Challenges

Big data poses several challenges that require specialized tools and techniques for effective processing and analysis. Some of the key challenges include:

- **Volume**: Big data typically involves massive volumes of data that cannot be handled by traditional databases or tools.

- **Variety**: Data comes in various formats, including structured, semi-structured, and unstructured data. Processing this diverse data requires flexibility.

- **Velocity**: Data is generated and updated rapidly in real-time, necessitating fast processing and analysis.

- **Veracity**: Big data can be noisy, incomplete, or inaccurate, making it challenging to derive meaningful insights.

Java for Big Data Processing

Java is well-suited for big data processing due to its characteristics:

- **Scalability**: Java applications can be easily scaled horizontally by adding more machines to the cluster, making it suitable for handling large volumes of data.

- **Versatility**: Java supports a wide range of data processing frameworks and libraries, including Apache Hadoop, Apache Spark, Apache Flink, and more.

- **Performance**: Java's strong performance makes it suitable for processing and analyzing data quickly and efficiently.

Apache Hadoop and Java

Apache Hadoop is one of the most widely-used frameworks for big data processing, and it is written in Java. Hadoop provides a distributed file system (HDFS) and a distributed processing framework (MapReduce) that allows Java applications to process vast amounts of data across clusters of machines.

Here's how Java is used with Apache Hadoop:

1. **MapReduce**: Java developers write MapReduce programs to process data in parallel across a Hadoop cluster. The framework handles tasks like data distribution, task scheduling, and fault tolerance.

2. **Hive and Pig**: Hive and Pig are data query and scripting languages built on top of Hadoop. Java developers can use these tools to write SQL-like queries and data transformations for big data.

3. **HBase**: HBase is a NoSQL database that runs on top of Hadoop and is written in Java. It is suitable for storing and retrieving large volumes of data.

Apache Spark and Java

Apache Spark, another powerful big data processing framework, provides native support for Java. Java developers can leverage Spark's in-memory processing capabilities for faster data analysis. Spark also offers libraries like MLlib for machine learning and Spark Streaming for real-time data processing, making it a versatile choice for various big data tasks.

Java Libraries for Big Data

In addition to Hadoop and Spark, Java has a rich ecosystem of libraries and tools for big data processing. Some notable libraries and frameworks include:

- **Apache Kafka**: A distributed streaming platform that is often used for real-time data ingestion.

- **Apache Flink**: A stream processing framework for big data analytics and event-driven applications.

- **Elasticsearch**: A search and analytics engine for real-time and batch data analysis.

- **Spring for Apache Hadoop**: A project that simplifies the development of Hadoop applications using the Spring Framework.

Java's compatibility with these tools and frameworks makes it a preferred choice for organizations dealing with big data challenges. Java developers can build scalable and high-performance big data applications to extract valuable insights from massive datasets.

13.5 Real-Time Data Streaming with Kafka

In the realm of big data and real-time data processing, Apache Kafka has emerged as a powerful and popular technology. Kafka is an open-source distributed streaming platform that is designed for high-throughput, fault-tolerant, and real-time data streaming. In this section, we'll explore how Kafka is used for real-time data streaming with Java.

Introduction to Apache Kafka

Apache Kafka is often described as a distributed commit log or a distributed messaging system. It is designed to handle the following key requirements:

- **Publish and Subscribe**: Kafka allows producers to publish data, and consumers can subscribe to specific topics to receive and process this data.

- **Real-Time**: Kafka provides low-latency, real-time data streaming capabilities. It is capable of handling millions of events per second.

- **Fault Tolerance**: Kafka is highly fault-tolerant. It replicates data across multiple nodes, ensuring data durability.

- **Scalability**: Kafka is horizontally scalable, meaning you can add more brokers and partitions to handle increased data loads.

Kafka Components

Kafka consists of the following components:

1. **Producer**: Producers are responsible for publishing data to Kafka topics. In Java, you can use the Kafka Producer API to create producer applications.

2. **Broker**: Kafka brokers are the Kafka servers that store and manage data. They are responsible for receiving data from producers and serving data to consumers.

3. **Topic**: Topics are logical channels to which data is published by producers. Topics can have multiple partitions to parallelize data distribution.

4. **Consumer**: Consumers subscribe to topics and process the data. Java applications can use the Kafka Consumer API to consume data from Kafka topics.

5. **Zookeeper**: Kafka relies on Apache ZooKeeper for distributed coordination and management of brokers and topics. However, ZooKeeper's role in Kafka is diminishing with newer Kafka releases.

Kafka and Java

Java is one of the primary programming languages used for building Kafka producers and consumers. Kafka provides an official Java client that simplifies interactions with Kafka clusters. Here's how you can create Kafka producers and consumers using Java:

Creating a Kafka Producer in Java

```java
import org.apache.kafka.clients.producer.*;

public class KafkaProducerExample {
    public static void main(String[] args) {
        String bootstrapServers = "localhost:9092";
        String topic = "my-topic";

        Properties properties = new Properties();
        properties.setProperty(ProducerConfig.BOOTSTRAP_SERVERS_CONFIG, boots
trapServers);
        properties.setProperty(ProducerConfig.KEY_SERIALIZER_CLASS_CONFIG, St
```

```java
ringSerializer.class.getName());
        properties.setProperty(ProducerConfig.VALUE_SERIALIZER_CLASS_CONFIG,
StringSerializer.class.getName());

        Producer<String, String> producer = new KafkaProducer<>(properties);

        ProducerRecord<String, String> record = new ProducerRecord<>(topic, "
key", "value");

        producer.send(record, new Callback() {
            public void onCompletion(RecordMetadata metadata, Exception e) {
                if (e == null) {
                    System.out.println("Message sent successfully to partitio
n " + metadata.partition());
                } else {
                    e.printStackTrace();
                }
            }
        });

        producer.close();
    }
}
```

Creating a Kafka Consumer in Java

```java
import org.apache.kafka.clients.consumer.*;
import java.util.Collections;

public class KafkaConsumerExample {
    public static void main(String[] args) {
        String bootstrapServers = "localhost:9092";
        String groupId = "my-group";
        String topic = "my-topic";

        Properties properties = new Properties();
        properties.setProperty(ConsumerConfig.BOOTSTRAP_SERVERS_CONFIG, boots
trapServers);
        properties.setProperty(ConsumerConfig.GROUP_ID_CONFIG, groupId);
        properties.setProperty(ConsumerConfig.KEY_DESERIALIZER_CLASS_CONFIG,
StringDeserializer.class.getName());
        properties.setProperty(ConsumerConfig.VALUE_DESERIALIZER_CLASS_CONFIG
, StringDeserializer.class.getName());

        KafkaConsumer<String, String> consumer = new KafkaConsumer<>(properti
es);

        consumer.subscribe(Collections.singletonList(topic));

        while (true) {
```

```
        ConsumerRecords<String, String> records = consumer.poll(Duration.
ofMillis(100));
        for (ConsumerRecord<String, String> record : records) {
            System.out.println("Received message: " + record.value());
        }
    }
  }
}
```

These code snippets demonstrate how to create a Kafka producer and consumer in Java, allowing you to publish and consume real-time data streams efficiently. Kafka's capabilities make it a valuable tool for building real-time data processing pipelines and applications.

14.1 Cloud Computing Basics

Cloud computing has revolutionized the way businesses and individuals manage and access computing resources. In this section, we will explore the fundamental concepts and key aspects of cloud computing.

What is Cloud Computing?

At its core, cloud computing refers to the delivery of various services and resources over the internet. These services include but are not limited to computing power, storage, databases, networking, software, and more. Instead of owning and maintaining physical hardware and software, users can access and utilize these resources on a pay-as-you-go basis, typically through a cloud service provider.

Key Characteristics of Cloud Computing

1. **On-Demand Self-Service**: Users can provision and manage resources as needed, without requiring human intervention from the service provider.

2. **Broad Network Access**: Cloud services are accessible over the internet from a variety of devices, such as laptops, smartphones, and tablets.

3. **Resource Pooling**: Cloud providers pool and allocate resources to serve multiple customers. Resources are dynamically assigned based on demand.

4. **Rapid Elasticity**: Cloud resources can be scaled up or down quickly to accommodate changing workloads, ensuring efficient resource utilization.

5. **Measured Service**: Cloud usage is metered, allowing users to pay only for the resources they consume. This is often referred to as a "pay-as-you-go" model.

Service Models

Cloud computing offers various service models, each catering to different user needs. The three primary service models are:

1. **Infrastructure as a Service (IaaS)**: IaaS provides virtualized computing resources over the internet. Users can rent virtual machines, storage, and networking components. This model offers maximum flexibility and control over the underlying infrastructure.

2. **Platform as a Service (PaaS)**: PaaS provides a platform for developers to build, deploy, and manage applications without worrying about the underlying infrastructure. It typically includes development tools, databases, and runtime environments.

3. **Software as a Service (SaaS)**: SaaS delivers software applications over the internet. Users can access these applications through a web browser without needing to install or maintain them. Common examples include email services and office productivity suites.

Deployment Models

Cloud computing can be deployed in different ways to meet specific requirements:

1. **Public Cloud**: Services and resources are owned and operated by a cloud service provider and made available to the general public. Examples of public cloud providers include Amazon Web Services (AWS), Microsoft Azure, and Google Cloud Platform (GCP).

2. **Private Cloud**: Cloud infrastructure is exclusively used by a single organization. It can be hosted on-premises or by a third-party provider. Private clouds offer greater control and security but may require higher upfront costs.

3. **Hybrid Cloud**: Hybrid cloud combines public and private cloud environments, allowing data and applications to be shared between them. This flexibility enables organizations to optimize resource usage and data placement.

4. **Multi-Cloud**: Multi-cloud involves using services from multiple cloud providers. Organizations choose this approach to avoid vendor lock-in and leverage the strengths of different providers for various purposes.

Benefits of Cloud Computing

Cloud computing offers numerous advantages, including:

- Cost Efficiency: Cloud services eliminate the need for upfront hardware investments and reduce operational costs.

- Scalability: Cloud resources can be easily scaled up or down to accommodate changing workloads.

- Flexibility: Users have access to a wide range of services and can choose the most suitable ones for their needs.

- Accessibility: Cloud services can be accessed from anywhere with an internet connection.

- Disaster Recovery: Cloud providers typically offer robust backup and disaster recovery options.

- Security: Cloud providers invest heavily in security measures, often providing better security than on-premises solutions.

In this digital age, cloud computing has become an essential technology for businesses and individuals alike, enabling innovation, agility, and cost-effective IT solutions.

14.2 Deploying Java Applications to the Cloud

Once you have developed a Java application, you may want to deploy it to the cloud to make it accessible to users worldwide. This section will guide you through the process of deploying Java applications to cloud platforms like Amazon Web Services (AWS), Microsoft Azure, and Google Cloud Platform (GCP).

Prerequisites

Before deploying your Java application to the cloud, you need to have the following prerequisites in place:

1. **Cloud Account**: Sign up for an account with the cloud provider of your choice. Most providers offer a free tier with limited resources to get started.

2. **Java Development Environment**: Ensure that you have Java Development Kit (JDK) installed on your local machine.

3. **Packaged Application**: Your Java application should be packaged into a deployable format. This typically involves creating a JAR (Java Archive) file or a WAR (Web Application Archive) file for web applications.

Deploying to Amazon Web Services (AWS)

AWS offers a range of services for deploying Java applications, including Amazon Elastic Beanstalk, AWS Lambda, and Amazon EC2. Here's a high-level overview of the deployment process:

1. **Create an AWS Account**: If you don't already have an AWS account, sign up for one.

2. **Prepare Your Application**: Package your Java application into a deployable format (e.g., JAR or WAR).

3. **Choose a Deployment Service**: Select the AWS service that best fits your application's needs. For example, use Elastic Beanstalk for web applications, Lambda for serverless functions, or EC2 for more control over infrastructure.

4. **Upload and Deploy**: Upload your application package to AWS and deploy it using the chosen service. AWS provides detailed documentation and tutorials for each service.

Deploying to Microsoft Azure

Azure offers various services for deploying Java applications, such as Azure App Service, Azure Functions, and Azure Virtual Machines. Here's an overview of the deployment process on Azure:

1. **Create an Azure Account**: If you don't have an Azure account, sign up for one.

2. **Package Your Application**: Package your Java application into a deployable format, such as a JAR or WAR file.

3. **Choose a Deployment Service**: Select the Azure service that aligns with your application's requirements. Azure App Service is suitable for web applications, while Azure Functions are designed for serverless computing.

4. **Upload and Deploy**: Upload your application package to Azure and deploy it using the chosen service. Azure provides detailed documentation and guides for each service.

Deploying to Google Cloud Platform (GCP)

Google Cloud Platform offers services like Google App Engine, Google Kubernetes Engine (GKE), and Google Compute Engine for deploying Java applications. Here's a general overview of the deployment process on GCP:

1. **Create a GCP Account**: If you don't already have one, sign up for a Google Cloud Platform account.

2. **Package Your Application**: Package your Java application into a deployable format, such as a JAR or WAR file.

3. **Select a Deployment Service**: Choose the GCP service that suits your application's needs. App Engine is ideal for web applications, GKE provides container orchestration, and Compute Engine offers virtual machines.

4. **Upload and Deploy**: Upload your application package to GCP and deploy it using the chosen service. GCP offers comprehensive documentation and tutorials for each service.

Continuous Integration and Deployment (CI/CD)

For a streamlined development and deployment workflow, consider implementing Continuous Integration and Continuous Deployment (CI/CD) practices. CI/CD pipelines automate the testing and deployment of your Java applications to the cloud whenever changes are made to the codebase. Popular CI/CD tools like Jenkins, Travis CI, and CircleCI can integrate seamlessly with cloud platforms to facilitate this process.

By following these steps and leveraging the cloud services provided by AWS, Azure, or GCP, you can easily deploy your Java applications to the cloud, making them accessible to users worldwide with scalability and reliability.

14.3 Amazon Web Services (AWS) and Java

Amazon Web Services (AWS) is one of the leading cloud service providers, offering a wide range of services that cater to Java developers. In this section, we'll explore some of the key AWS services that are commonly used in Java application development and deployment.

Amazon Elastic Beanstalk

Amazon Elastic Beanstalk is a Platform as a Service (PaaS) offering that simplifies the deployment of Java applications. It provides a platform for running web applications, including those built using Java, without the need to manage the underlying infrastructure. Here's how to get started with Elastic Beanstalk for Java applications:

1. **Create an Elastic Beanstalk Environment**: Use the AWS Management Console or the AWS Command Line Interface (CLI) to create an Elastic Beanstalk environment. You can specify the Java version and platform you want to use.

2. **Upload Your Application**: Package your Java application into a WAR (Web Application Archive) file and upload it to your Elastic Beanstalk environment.

3. **Configure Environment Variables**: Use the Elastic Beanstalk console to configure environment variables, such as database connection strings or API keys, that your Java application may require.

4. **Deploy Your Application**: Deploy your Java application to the Elastic Beanstalk environment. AWS handles the deployment, scaling, and monitoring of your application.

AWS Lambda

AWS Lambda is a serverless computing service that allows you to run code in response to events without provisioning or managing servers. You can use AWS Lambda to execute Java code in a serverless fashion. Here's how to use AWS Lambda with Java:

1. **Create a Lambda Function**: Use the AWS Lambda console to create a new Lambda function. You can choose Java as the runtime.

2. **Upload Your Java JAR**: Package your Java code into a JAR file and upload it as the deployment package for your Lambda function.

3. **Define Triggers**: Configure the triggers that will invoke your Lambda function. Triggers can include AWS services like Amazon S3, Amazon API Gateway, or AWS IoT.

4. **Set Up Permissions**: Define the AWS Identity and Access Management (IAM) roles and permissions required for your Lambda function to access other AWS resources.

5. **Monitoring and Logging**: Use AWS CloudWatch to monitor and log the execution of your Lambda functions. You can set up alarms and dashboards for better visibility.

Amazon RDS

Amazon Relational Database Service (RDS) is a managed database service that supports various database engines, including MySQL, PostgreSQL, Oracle, and Microsoft SQL Server. Java applications often require databases for data storage. You can easily connect your Java application to an Amazon RDS instance by following these steps:

1. **Create an RDS Instance**: Use the AWS RDS console to create a new database instance, choosing the database engine that suits your application.

2. **Configure Security Groups**: Set up security groups to control access to your RDS instance. You can define rules to allow traffic from your Java application's security group.

3. **Database Connection**: In your Java application, use JDBC (Java Database Connectivity) to establish a connection to the RDS database. Provide the database endpoint, credentials, and other necessary details.

4. **Data Modeling and Queries**: Design your database schema and write SQL queries to interact with the database. You can use Java libraries like Hibernate or JPA for object-relational mapping.

5. **Backups and Maintenance**: RDS automates backups, patching, and routine maintenance tasks, reducing the operational overhead.

Amazon S3

Amazon Simple Storage Service (S3) is an object storage service that can be used to store and retrieve files, images, and other data in your Java applications. To work with S3 in Java:

1. **Create an S3 Bucket**: Use the AWS S3 console to create a bucket where you can store your data objects.

2. **AWS SDK for Java**: Utilize the AWS SDK for Java to interact with S3 from your Java code. You can upload, download, and manage objects programmatically.

3. **Access Control**: Configure bucket policies and access control lists (ACLs) to control who can access and manipulate objects in your S3 bucket.

4. **Versioning and Lifecycle Policies**: S3 supports versioning and lifecycle policies, allowing you to manage object versions and automate data archiving or deletion.

These are just a few of the AWS services that can enhance your Java applications. AWS offers extensive documentation and resources for Java developers to help you leverage the cloud's scalability and flexibility in your projects.

14.4 Microsoft Azure and Java

Microsoft Azure is a popular cloud computing platform that provides a wide range of services for building, deploying, and managing Java applications. In this section, we'll explore how Azure can be used in conjunction with Java for various cloud-based scenarios.

Azure App Service

Azure App Service is a platform-as-a-service (PaaS) offering that allows you to build, host, and scale web applications in various programming languages, including Java. Here's how you can use Azure App Service with Java:

1. **Create an Azure Web App**: Use the Azure Portal or Azure CLI to create a new web app. You can select the Java runtime and version that your application requires.

2. **Deploy Your Java Application**: Package your Java application into a WAR (Web Application Archive) or JAR (Java Archive) file and deploy it to your Azure Web App. You can use Git, FTP, or Azure DevOps for deployment.

3. **Scaling and Load Balancing**: Azure App Service provides automatic scaling based on demand. You can configure auto-scaling rules to ensure your Java application can handle varying workloads.

4. **Integration with Azure Services**: Azure Web Apps can easily integrate with other Azure services like Azure SQL Database, Azure Storage, and Azure Cosmos DB. This makes it simple to add data storage, caching, and messaging to your Java application.

Azure Functions

Azure Functions is a serverless computing service that enables you to run event-driven code without managing infrastructure. You can use Azure Functions to execute Java code in response to events from various Azure services and triggers. Here's how to get started with Azure Functions in Java:

1. **Create an Azure Function**: Use the Azure Functions portal or Azure CLI to create a new function app. You can choose Java as the runtime stack.

2. **Develop and Deploy**: Write your Java code for the function, package it into a JAR file, and deploy it to your function app. You can define triggers and bindings to specify when and how your function runs.

3. **Event-Driven Processing**: Azure Functions can be triggered by various Azure services such as Azure Blob Storage, Azure Event Hubs, or Azure Service Bus. Your Java code responds to these events.

4. **Serverless Scalability**: Azure Functions automatically scales to accommodate incoming events, ensuring your Java code runs efficiently.

Azure Spring Cloud

Azure Spring Cloud is a fully managed service jointly developed by Microsoft and VMware. It is designed to simplify the deployment, scaling, and management of Spring Boot applications. Here's how you can use Azure Spring Cloud with Java:

1. **Create an Azure Spring Cloud Service**: Use the Azure Portal or Azure CLI to provision an Azure Spring Cloud instance.

2. **Deploy Spring Boot Apps**: Package your Spring Boot applications as JAR files and deploy them to Azure Spring Cloud. You can use the Azure CLI, Maven, or Gradle for deployment.

3. **Scaling and Load Balancing**: Azure Spring Cloud provides built-in load balancing and scaling capabilities. You can easily adjust the number of instances based on your application's needs.

4. **Integration with Azure Services**: Azure Spring Cloud integrates seamlessly with Azure services like Azure Database for MySQL, Azure Service Bus, and Azure Monitor.

5. **Monitoring and Diagnostics**: Azure Spring Cloud offers monitoring and diagnostic tools to help you troubleshoot and optimize your Java applications.

These are some of the key Azure services that enable Java developers to build, deploy, and manage applications in the cloud. Azure provides robust tools, documentation, and support for Java development, making it a viable choice for cloud-based solutions.

14.5 Google Cloud Platform (GCP) and Java

Google Cloud Platform (GCP) is a suite of cloud computing services offered by Google. It provides a range of tools and services for building, deploying, and managing Java applications in the cloud. In this section, we'll explore how GCP can be used with Java for various cloud-based scenarios.

Google App Engine

Google App Engine is a platform-as-a-service (PaaS) offering that allows you to build and deploy web applications and APIs with ease. Java is one of the supported programming languages for App Engine. Here's how you can use Google App Engine with Java:

1. **Create a New App**: Use the Google Cloud Console to create a new App Engine application. You can specify the runtime environment for Java.

2. **Develop Your Java Application**: Write your Java web application using frameworks like Spring Boot or servlets. You can use the Google Cloud SDK to test your app locally.

3. **Deployment**: Use the `gcloud` command-line tool to deploy your Java application to App Engine. Google provides a standard runtime and a flexible runtime for custom configurations.

4. **Scaling**: App Engine automatically handles application scaling based on incoming traffic. You can configure scaling settings to suit your needs.

5. **Data Storage**: GCP provides several options for data storage, including Cloud SQL for relational databases, Cloud Datastore for NoSQL databases, and Cloud Storage for file storage.

Google Kubernetes Engine (GKE)

Google Kubernetes Engine is a managed Kubernetes service that allows you to deploy, manage, and scale containerized applications using Google's infrastructure. You can run Java applications in containers on GKE. Here's how to use GKE with Java:

1. **Create a GKE Cluster**: Use the Google Cloud Console or `gcloud` command-line tool to create a GKE cluster.

2. **Containerize Your Java Application**: Package your Java application into a Docker container. You can use tools like Docker or Google Cloud Build to create container images.

3. **Deploy to GKE**: Deploy your containerized Java application to GKE using Kubernetes manifests or Helm charts. Kubernetes provides features for load balancing and scaling.

4. **Scaling and Load Balancing**: GKE allows you to scale your application horizontally by adding more replicas. Load balancing is managed by Kubernetes.

5. **Integration with GCP Services**: GKE easily integrates with other GCP services such as Cloud SQL, Cloud Pub/Sub, and Bigtable.

Google Cloud Functions

Google Cloud Functions is a serverless computing service that enables you to run event-driven code in response to various events. While Java is not natively supported, you can use Node.js or Python to create functions that interact with Java applications. Here's how it works:

1. **Create a Function**: Use Node.js or Python to create a Cloud Function that listens for events like HTTP requests, Cloud Pub/Sub messages, or changes in Cloud Storage.

2. **Invoke Java Code**: When an event triggers your Cloud Function, you can use it to invoke Java code running in another environment, such as a virtual machine or a container.

3. **Data Processing**: Cloud Functions can be used to process data and trigger actions in your Java applications. For example, you can use it for real-time data processing.

4. **Serverless Scaling**: Google Cloud Functions automatically scales to handle incoming events, ensuring your Java code is executed efficiently.

These are some of the ways you can leverage Google Cloud Platform for Java application development and deployment. GCP provides a wide range of services, including data analytics, machine learning, and IoT, making it a comprehensive platform for cloud-based solutions using Java.

Chapter 15: Java Best Practices

Chapter 15: Java Best Practices

Section 15.1: Code Style and Conventions

In software development, adhering to consistent code style and conventions is crucial for writing clean, maintainable, and readable code. Java is no exception, and it has established conventions and best practices that help developers write code that is easier to understand and collaborate on. This section explores the importance of code style and conventions in Java programming.

15.1.1 Why Code Style Matters

Code style is not just about aesthetics; it significantly impacts code quality, maintainability, and collaboration among developers. Here are some key reasons why code style matters:

1. **Readability:** A consistent code style makes code easier to read and understand. When developers follow the same conventions, it becomes simpler for anyone to grasp the code's structure and purpose.

2. **Maintainability:** Well-organized and consistently styled code is easier to maintain. Developers can quickly locate and fix issues, make enhancements, or extend functionality without getting lost in messy code.

3. **Collaboration:** In a team environment, everyone following the same code style ensures that team members can work seamlessly on different parts of a project. It reduces friction caused by style disagreements and promotes efficient collaboration.

4. **Reduced Errors:** A consistent code style helps prevent common errors and bugs. When everyone uses the same patterns and practices, it's less likely that code will contain hidden issues.

15.1.2 Java Code Conventions

Java has established code conventions outlined in the "Code Conventions for the Java Programming Language" document provided by Oracle. These conventions cover various aspects of code, including:

- **Naming Conventions:** Guidelines for naming classes, methods, variables, constants, and packages.
- **Formatting:** Rules for code indentation, line length, and spacing.
- **Comments:** Recommendations for adding meaningful comments to code.
- **Braces:** Guidelines for placing braces and indentation in code blocks.
- **Imports:** How to organize and format import statements.
- **Annotations:** Best practices for using annotations.

Developers are encouraged to follow these conventions to ensure consistency across Java projects. Many Integrated Development Environments (IDEs) provide automatic code formatting and inspections to help developers adhere to these conventions.

15.1.3 Tools for Enforcing Code Style

To maintain code style and conventions, developers can leverage various tools and plugins. Some popular options include:

- **Checkstyle:** A tool that checks code against coding standards and provides configurable rules for code style.

- **FindBugs:** A static code analysis tool that identifies potential bugs in Java code, including style-related issues.

- **IDE Plugins:** Integrated Development Environments like IntelliJ IDEA and Eclipse offer plugins that help enforce code style and formatting as you write code.

In conclusion, following code style and conventions is essential for writing maintainable and readable Java code. By adhering to established guidelines and using tools, developers can ensure consistency and reduce common coding errors, leading to higher-quality software.

Section 15.2: Code Reviews and Code Quality Tools

Code reviews are an integral part of maintaining code quality in Java projects. They involve a systematic examination of source code by peers to identify issues, ensure adherence to coding standards, and improve overall software quality. Additionally, code quality tools can automate some aspects of code review and analysis, making the process more efficient and effective.

15.2.1 Importance of Code Reviews

Code reviews offer several benefits:

1. **Error Detection:** Code reviews help catch bugs, logic errors, and issues early in the development process, reducing the cost and effort required to fix them later.

2. **Consistency:** Code reviews ensure that code follows coding standards and conventions, leading to consistent and readable code.

3. **Knowledge Sharing:** They provide an opportunity for knowledge transfer among team members, allowing less experienced developers to learn from their peers.

4. **Improved Design:** Code reviews can lead to discussions on code design, resulting in better, more maintainable software architecture.

5. **Increased Confidence:** A well-reviewed codebase instills confidence in its reliability and robustness.

15.2.2 Conducting Code Reviews

Here are some best practices for conducting effective code reviews:

- **Set Clear Objectives:** Define the goals of the code review, whether it's finding defects, ensuring code quality, or validating design decisions.

- **Review in Small Chunks:** Review smaller sections of code at a time to maintain focus and provide meaningful feedback.

- **Use Code Review Checklists:** Develop checklists based on coding standards, best practices, and project-specific requirements to guide reviewers.

- **Provide Constructive Feedback:** Offer specific, actionable feedback rather than vague or negative comments.

- **Balance Positive and Negative Feedback:** Acknowledge good practices alongside areas for improvement to maintain a positive atmosphere.

- **Discuss, Don't Dictate:** Encourage discussions and suggestions rather than imposing changes. Code reviews should be collaborative.

- **Consider Performance and Scalability:** Assess code for potential performance bottlenecks or scalability issues.

15.2.3 Code Quality Tools

Code quality tools automate the code review process to some extent and help identify issues that might be overlooked during manual reviews. Some popular code quality tools for Java include:

- **SonarQube:** A platform that performs static code analysis, detects code smells, bugs, and security vulnerabilities.

- **Checkstyle:** As mentioned earlier, it checks code against coding standards and enforces style conventions.

- **FindBugs and PMD:** Static analysis tools that identify potential issues and enforce coding standards.

- **JUnit and TestNG:** Testing frameworks for automating unit tests, ensuring code correctness.

- **JaCoCo:** A code coverage tool that measures how much of the codebase is covered by tests.

- **Jenkins and Travis CI:** Continuous integration tools that automate the build and testing process.

Incorporating these tools into the development pipeline can significantly improve code quality and reduce the burden of manual code reviews.

In summary, code reviews and code quality tools play a vital role in maintaining high-quality Java codebases. By conducting thorough reviews and leveraging automated analysis tools, development teams can ensure that their software is reliable, maintainable, and adheres to coding standards.

Section 15.3: Documentation and Comments

Effective documentation and comments are essential for understanding and maintaining Java code. Well-documented code not only helps the original developers but also benefits others who work on the codebase, including future maintainers. In this section, we'll explore the importance of documentation and provide best practices for writing comments in Java.

15.3.1 Importance of Documentation

Documentation serves several crucial purposes:

1. **Code Understanding:** It provides context and explanations, helping developers understand how code works and why certain decisions were made.

2. **Maintenance:** Good documentation makes it easier to maintain and extend the codebase because developers can quickly grasp the code's purpose and functionality.

3. **Collaboration:** Documentation facilitates collaboration among team members by making it clear how various components interact and how to use them.

4. **Onboarding:** New team members can ramp up faster with well-documented code, reducing the learning curve.

15.3.2 Writing Effective Comments

Here are some best practices for writing comments in Java:

- **Use Clear and Concise Language:** Write comments in a clear, concise, and natural language. Avoid jargon or overly technical terms.

- **Explain the "Why":** Don't just describe "what" the code does; explain "why" it does it. This helps others understand the rationale behind design decisions.

- **Header Comments:** Include a header comment at the beginning of each class or method, summarizing its purpose and usage.

- **In-line Comments:** Use in-line comments sparingly, focusing on complex or non-intuitive code sections. Over-commenting can clutter the code.

- **Update Comments:** Remember to update comments when you modify code to keep them in sync with the code's current state.

- **Use Documentation Tools:** Java provides tools like Javadoc, which generates documentation from specially formatted comments. Take advantage of these tools for generating API documentation.

15.3.3 Javadoc Comments

Javadoc is a tool that generates HTML documentation from specially formatted comments in Java source code. It's commonly used for documenting classes, methods, fields, and packages. Here's an example of a Javadoc comment:

```java
/**
 * This is a Javadoc comment for the MyClass class.
 *
 * @author John Doe
 * @version 1.0
 */
public class MyClass {
    /**
     * This is a Javadoc comment for the add method.
     *
     * @param a The first integer.
     * @param b The second integer.
     * @return The sum of a and b.
     */
    public int add(int a, int b) {
        return a + b;
    }
}
```

In this example, the Javadoc comment provides information about the class and its add method, including authorship, version, parameters, and return value. This documentation is then processed by the Javadoc tool to generate a comprehensive HTML documentation page for the class and its members.

By following Javadoc conventions, you can generate professional and consistent documentation for your Java projects, making it easier for developers to understand and use your code.

In conclusion, effective documentation and comments are vital for maintaining Java codebases. Well-documented code helps developers understand, maintain, and collaborate on projects more efficiently. Leveraging tools like Javadoc can streamline the documentation process and ensure that your code is well-documented and accessible to others.

Section 15.4: Refactoring and Code Smells

Refactoring is the process of improving the structure, readability, and maintainability of your code without changing its external behavior. It's an essential practice for keeping your codebase healthy and efficient. In this section, we'll explore the concept of refactoring and common code smells that indicate when refactoring is needed.

15.4.1 What Is Refactoring?

Refactoring is a disciplined technique for restructuring existing code. Its primary goals are to make code easier to understand, modify, and extend while preserving the code's external behavior. Refactoring should be an integral part of the development process and not considered as a separate activity.

Common reasons for refactoring include:

1. **Code Duplication:** When the same or similar code appears in multiple places, it can lead to maintenance issues. Refactoring can consolidate duplicate code into reusable functions or classes.

2. **Complexity:** Code that is overly complex can be challenging to understand and prone to bugs. Refactoring simplifies code, breaking it into smaller, more manageable pieces.

3. **Inefficiency:** Identifying and eliminating performance bottlenecks through refactoring can lead to faster and more efficient code.

4. **Readability:** Code that is hard to read, with poor naming and inconsistent style, can be refactored to improve its clarity.

15.4.2 Common Code Smells

Code smells are specific patterns in code that indicate potential issues. Recognizing these smells is the first step in identifying areas that need refactoring. Here are some common code smells:

- **Duplicated Code:** Repeated code blocks or similar code segments in different places.

- **Long Methods:** Methods that are excessively long and perform too many tasks. They are hard to understand and maintain.

- **Large Classes:** Classes that have grown too large and handle too many responsibilities. These classes are often difficult to modify.

- **Primitive Obsession:** Excessive use of primitive data types (e.g., int, String) instead of creating custom classes to represent concepts.

- **Long Parameter Lists:** Methods with a large number of parameters, which can make calling and understanding the method challenging.

- **Conditional Complexity:** Methods or classes with deeply nested if statements or switch cases. This indicates complex control flow.

- **Inconsistent Naming:** Inconsistent variable, method, or class names that make the code harder to follow.

- **Comments:** Excessive comments that try to explain complex or convoluted code instead of refactoring for clarity.

15.4.3 Refactoring Techniques

There are various refactoring techniques you can apply to address code smells. Some common refactoring techniques include:

- **Extract Method:** Break down a long method into smaller, more focused methods.

- **Extract Class:** Move a group of related fields and methods into a new class.

- **Rename:** Choose clear and descriptive names for variables, methods, and classes.

- **Remove Duplication:** Consolidate duplicated code into reusable functions or classes.

- **Simplify Conditionals:** Simplify complex conditional statements by using early returns or polymorphism.

- **Introduce Explaining Variable:** Create well-named variables to explain complex expressions.

- **Inline Method:** Replace a method call with its content for improved readability.

- **Split Loop:** Break a loop into multiple smaller loops to clarify its purpose.

- **Replace Conditional with Polymorphism:** Replace a series of if statements with polymorphic behavior.

- **Replace Magic Numbers with Named Constants:** Replace hardcoded values with named constants for improved code readability.

- **Encapsulate Fields:** Limit direct access to fields by providing getter and setter methods for better encapsulation.

Refactoring should be performed incrementally and accompanied by thorough testing to ensure that the code's behavior remains correct. Version control systems can help you track changes and revert to previous states if necessary.

In conclusion, refactoring is a fundamental practice for maintaining high-quality code. Recognizing code smells and applying appropriate refactoring techniques can lead to code that is more maintainable, readable, and efficient, ultimately making development and maintenance tasks easier and less error-prone.

Section 15.5: Building Maintainable Java Applications

Building maintainable Java applications is crucial for long-term success. As your project evolves, maintaining and enhancing your codebase becomes more challenging. In this section, we'll explore best practices and strategies for building Java applications that are easy to maintain.

15.5.1 Follow Coding Standards

Consistency in coding style and conventions is essential for maintainability. Adopt a set of coding standards or style guides, such as those provided by Google or Oracle. These guides cover naming conventions, code formatting, and best practices. Tools like Checkstyle and SonarQube can help enforce these standards automatically.

15.5.2 Modularize Your Code

Break your application into modular components with well-defined responsibilities. Use packages and classes to organize related code. Modularization enhances code readability and makes it easier to find and modify specific functionality.

15.5.3 Use Descriptive Naming

Choose meaningful and descriptive names for classes, methods, variables, and packages. Avoid cryptic abbreviations and single-letter variable names. Descriptive names make your code self-documenting and understandable to others.

15.5.4 Comment Thoughtfully

While code should be self-explanatory, well-placed comments can provide context and explain complex logic. Write comments that focus on "why" rather than "what." Avoid over-commenting, as excessive comments can become outdated and misleading.

15.5.5 Unit Testing

Adopt a test-driven development (TDD) approach. Write unit tests for your code to ensure that it behaves correctly. Automated tests catch regressions during development and make it safer to refactor code. Use frameworks like JUnit for unit testing.

15.5.6 Version Control

Use a version control system like Git to track changes to your codebase. Commit frequently and write meaningful commit messages. Branch your code for new features or bug fixes. Version control enables collaboration and provides a safety net for code changes.

15.5.7 Document Your Code

Provide documentation for your code, including Javadoc comments for classes and methods. Document public APIs thoroughly. Tools like JavaDoc generate documentation from comments, making it accessible to other developers.

15.5.8 Continuous Integration (CI)

Implement continuous integration (CI) to automate building, testing, and deployment processes. CI tools like Jenkins and Travis CI help catch integration issues early and ensure that your codebase is always in a working state.

15.5.9 Refactor Regularly

As discussed in the previous section, refactor your code to eliminate code smells and maintainability issues. Small, incremental refactorings are easier to manage than large, complex ones.

15.5.10 Keep Dependencies in Check

Manage your project's dependencies carefully. Use build tools like Maven or Gradle to specify and resolve dependencies. Regularly update dependencies to benefit from bug fixes and improvements. Be cautious about adding unnecessary dependencies that can bloat your project.

15.5.11 Error Handling

Implement robust error handling mechanisms. Use checked exceptions for recoverable errors and unchecked exceptions for unrecoverable errors. Provide meaningful error messages and log them for debugging purposes.

15.5.12 Monitor and Analyze

Implement logging and monitoring to track the health and performance of your application in production. Tools like Log4j and Prometheus can help you gather valuable insights into your application's behavior.

15.5.13 Plan for Maintenance

Acknowledge that software maintenance is an ongoing process. Allocate time for regular maintenance tasks, including bug fixes, security updates, and feature enhancements. A well-maintained application is less likely to become legacy software.

By following these best practices, you can build Java applications that are not only functional but also maintainable and adaptable to changing requirements. Building maintainability into your development process from the start will save you time and effort in the long run, ensuring that your application remains a valuable asset.

Chapter 16: Java in the Enterprise

Section 16.1: Java EE (Enterprise Edition)

Java Enterprise Edition (Java EE), now known as Jakarta EE, is a set of specifications that extend the Java SE (Standard Edition) platform to provide enterprise-level features. It offers a robust and scalable environment for developing and deploying enterprise applications. In this section, we'll explore the fundamentals of Java EE and its key components.

What is Java EE?

Java EE is designed to simplify the development of large-scale, distributed, and transactional enterprise applications. It provides a comprehensive set of APIs and services that address various enterprise concerns, such as security, transaction management, and scalability.

Key Components of Java EE

1. **Servlets and JSP (JavaServer Pages):** Servlets and JSPs are the building blocks of web applications in Java EE. Servlets handle HTTP requests and responses, while JSPs provide a way to create dynamic web content.

2. **Enterprise JavaBeans (EJB):** EJBs are server-side components used for implementing business logic in enterprise applications. They offer features like transaction management, security, and remote access.

3. **Java Persistence API (JPA):** JPA is a standard for object-relational mapping (ORM) in Java EE. It allows developers to work with relational databases using Java objects.

4. **Java Messaging Service (JMS):** JMS provides a messaging system for communication between distributed components. It supports both point-to-point and publish-subscribe messaging models.

5. **Java Naming and Directory Interface (JNDI):** JNDI is used for naming and directory services in Java EE. It allows applications to locate and access enterprise resources, such as EJBs and data sources, through a naming service.

6. **Java API for RESTful Web Services (JAX-RS):** JAX-RS enables the development of RESTful web services in Java EE. It simplifies the creation of web APIs that follow the REST architectural style.

7. **Contexts and Dependency Injection (CDI):** CDI is a framework for managing bean lifecycles and injecting dependencies. It promotes loose coupling and helps create more maintainable applications.

8. **Java Authentication and Authorization Service (JAAS):** JAAS provides a framework for user authentication and authorization in Java EE applications. It supports various authentication mechanisms and allows role-based access control.

To run Java EE applications, you need a compatible application server that implements the Java EE specifications. Some popular Java EE application servers include:

- **Apache TomEE**
- **WildFly (formerly JBoss)**
- **GlassFish**
- **Payara Server**
- **IBM WebSphere**

These servers provide the runtime environment for deploying and executing Java EE applications.

Java EE offers several advantages for enterprise application development:

- **Scalability:** Java EE applications can scale horizontally to handle increased load by adding more servers to a cluster.

- **Security:** Java EE provides a robust security framework with features like authentication, authorization, and secure communication.

- **Transaction Management:** It offers built-in support for managing transactions, ensuring data consistency in enterprise applications.

- **Portability:** Java EE applications are portable across different application servers, reducing vendor lock-in.

- **Resource Management:** Java EE simplifies the management of resources such as database connections and messaging resources.

Java EE has evolved over the years and continues to adapt to modern application development needs. Jakarta EE, the successor to Java EE, is the open-source version of the platform and is governed by the Eclipse Foundation. Jakarta EE maintains backward compatibility with Java EE while embracing modern technologies and practices.

Section 16.2: Enterprise Application Architecture

Enterprise application architecture is a critical aspect of designing and building robust, scalable, and maintainable software systems for large organizations. In this section, we'll explore the key principles and components of enterprise application architecture using Java EE.

Principles of Enterprise Application Architecture

1. **Modularity:** Enterprise applications should be modular, with well-defined components that encapsulate specific functionality. Modularity promotes code reusability and maintainability.

2. **Scalability:** Scalability is essential for handling increasing workloads. Enterprise applications should be designed to scale horizontally by adding more servers or nodes to a cluster.

3. **Reliability:** Reliability is crucial in enterprise settings. Applications should be fault-tolerant and capable of handling failures gracefully.

4. **Security:** Enterprise applications often deal with sensitive data. Security measures, such as authentication, authorization, and encryption, must be in place to protect data and resources.

5. **Performance:** Performance optimization is key. Applications should be designed to minimize latency and maximize throughput.

6. **Interoperability:** Enterprise applications frequently need to integrate with other systems. Standards-based communication protocols and data formats facilitate interoperability.

Common Components of Enterprise Application Architecture

1. **Presentation Layer:** This layer handles the user interface and presentation logic. In Java EE, Servlets and JavaServer Pages (JSP) are commonly used for web-based presentation.

2. **Business Logic Layer:** This layer contains the core business logic of the application. Enterprise JavaBeans (EJBs) are often used to implement business components in Java EE.

3. **Data Access Layer:** The data access layer is responsible for interacting with databases and other data sources. The Java Persistence API (JPA) is a standard Java EE component for ORM (Object-Relational Mapping).

4. **Integration Layer:** This layer deals with external systems and services. It includes components like Java Messaging Service (JMS) for asynchronous communication and Java API for RESTful Web Services (JAX-RS) for building and consuming web services.

5. **Security Layer:** Security components, such as Java Authentication and Authorization Service (JAAS), are used to enforce security policies.

Design patterns play a significant role in enterprise application development. Some common design patterns used in Java EE include:

- **Model-View-Controller (MVC):** MVC separates the presentation logic (View), application logic (Controller), and data (Model) to improve modularity and maintainability.

- **Service-Oriented Architecture (SOA):** SOA promotes the creation of reusable services that can be accessed over a network. Java EE supports SOA through technologies like JAX-RS.

- **Enterprise Integration Patterns (EIP):** EIP provides solutions for integrating different systems and handling messaging patterns. Java EE's JMS is aligned with EIP concepts.

- **Dependency Injection (DI):** DI is used for managing dependencies between components. Java EE includes Contexts and Dependency Injection (CDI) to facilitate DI.

Enterprise Application Servers

Enterprise applications are typically deployed on application servers that implement Java EE or Jakarta EE specifications. These servers provide the runtime environment for executing Java EE applications. Some popular enterprise application servers include WildFly, GlassFish, Payara Server, and Apache TomEE.

Conclusion

Effective enterprise application architecture is essential for building complex, scalable, and reliable systems. Java EE, with its comprehensive set of components and standards, provides a robust platform for developing enterprise-grade applications that meet the demands of modern organizations.

Section 16.3: Java Persistence API (JPA)

The Java Persistence API (JPA) is a key component of Java EE for simplifying database access and management in enterprise applications. It is an object-relational mapping (ORM) framework that allows developers to work with relational databases using Java objects. In this section, we'll explore JPA and its essential features.

Basics of JPA

JPA simplifies database interactions by mapping Java objects to database tables. It abstracts the underlying SQL queries and provides a more intuitive way to perform CRUD (Create,

Read, Update, Delete) operations. JPA is part of the Java EE specification, making it a standard choice for enterprise applications.

1. **Entity:** An entity in JPA is a Java class that represents a database table. Each instance of an entity class corresponds to a row in the table.

2. **EntityManager:** The EntityManager is a central interface in JPA that manages the lifecycle of entity instances. It handles tasks like persisting, querying, and removing entities.

3. **Persistence Unit:** A persistence unit is a configuration that defines which entities are managed by JPA and how the data source is accessed. It is typically configured in a persistence.xml file.

4. **JPQL (Java Persistence Query Language):** JPQL is a SQL-like query language used to query entities in a database-agnostic way. It operates on entity classes and fields rather than database tables and columns.

5. **Annotations:** JPA uses annotations to define the mapping between Java objects and database tables. Annotations like @Entity, @Table, @Id, and @Column are commonly used.

Basic JPA Workflow

Here's a simplified workflow of how JPA works in an enterprise application:

1. **Define Entity Classes:** Create Java classes annotated with @Entity to represent database tables. Define fields and relationships as needed.

2. **Configure Persistence Unit:** Create a persistence.xml file to configure the persistence unit, data source, and other JPA settings.

3. **Create EntityManager:** In your application code, obtain an instance of the EntityManager either through injection (CDI) or programmatically.

4. **CRUD Operations:** Use the EntityManager to perform CRUD operations on entity instances. For example, use persist() to create new entities, find() to retrieve entities by primary key, merge() to update entities, and remove() to delete entities.

5. **JPQL Queries:** Use JPQL queries to retrieve data from the database. JPQL queries are defined as strings and can be executed using the createQuery() method of EntityManager.

Example Code

Let's look at a simplified example of using JPA to define an entity and perform CRUD operations:

```java
@Entity
@Table(name = "employees")
public class Employee {
    @Id
    @GeneratedValue(strategy = GenerationType.IDENTITY)
    private Long id;

    @Column(name = "first_name")
    private String firstName;

    @Column(name = "last_name")
    private String lastName;

    // Getters and setters
}

// In your application code:

// Create and configure EntityManagerFactory
EntityManagerFactory emf = Persistence.createEntityManagerFactory("my-persist
ence-unit");

// Create EntityManager
EntityManager em = emf.createEntityManager();

// Create a new Employee
Employee employee = new Employee();
employee.setFirstName("John");
employee.setLastName("Doe");

// Persist the Employee to the database
em.getTransaction().begin();
em.persist(employee);
em.getTransaction().commit();

// Retrieve an Employee by ID
Employee retrievedEmployee = em.find(Employee.class, 1L);

// Update an Employee
em.getTransaction().begin();
retrievedEmployee.setLastName("Smith");
em.getTransaction().commit();

// Delete an Employee
em.getTransaction().begin();
em.remove(retrievedEmployee);
em.getTransaction().commit();

// Close EntityManager and EntityManagerFactory when done
```

```
em.close();
emf.close();
```

Conclusion

The Java Persistence API (JPA) simplifies database access in enterprise applications by
providing a high-level, object-oriented approach to working with relational databases. It
abstracts many of the complexities of JDBC and SQL, allowing developers to focus on
business logic and data modeling. JPA is a valuable tool for Java EE developers building
data-driven applications.

Section 16.4: Java Messaging Service (JMS)

The Java Messaging Service (JMS) is a Java API for creating, sending, receiving, and
processing messages between distributed applications. It is a key component in building
enterprise applications that require asynchronous communication and messaging patterns.
In this section, we'll explore JMS and its role in Java EE.

Key Concepts in JMS

1. Message Broker:

JMS typically operates with the help of a message broker, which acts as an intermediary
between message producers and consumers. The broker manages the routing and delivery
of messages, ensuring they reach the correct destinations.

2. JMS Providers:

JMS is an API specification, and there are various JMS providers available, such as Apache
ActiveMQ, IBM MQ, and RabbitMQ. These providers implement the JMS API and provide the
infrastructure needed for message queuing and publish-subscribe mechanisms.

3. Messaging Models:

JMS supports two main messaging models: point-to-point (queue-based) and publish-
subscribe (topic-based). - **Point-to-Point (P2P):** In this model, messages are sent to a
specific queue, and only one consumer can receive each message. It is suitable for scenarios
where one message should be processed by one receiver. - **Publish-Subscribe (Pub-Sub):**
In this model, messages are sent to a topic, and multiple subscribers can receive copies of
the message. It is useful for broadcasting messages to multiple consumers.

4. Message Types:

JMS supports various message types, including TextMessage (for plain text), ObjectMessage
(for serializable Java objects), and MapMessage (for key-value pairs).

Basic JMS Workflow

Here's a simplified workflow of how JMS works in an enterprise application:

1. **Create JMS Resources:** Set up JMS resources such as connection factories, destinations (queues or topics), and message listeners. This configuration is typically done in a Java EE application server or JMS provider.

2. **Produce Messages:** Create message producers (senders) that create and send messages to JMS destinations. Producers use connection factories to establish connections and sessions for message production.

3. **Consume Messages:** Create message consumers (receivers) that listen to JMS destinations for incoming messages. Consumers register message listeners to process received messages asynchronously.

4. **Handle Messages:** As messages arrive at their destinations, the registered message listeners handle them. The message processing logic can be customized to suit the application's needs.

Example Code

Let's look at a simplified example of using JMS with Apache ActiveMQ, a popular JMS provider, to send and receive messages:

```java
// Create JNDI context and lookup JMS resources (configuration may vary by JM
S provider)
Context context = new InitialContext();
ConnectionFactory connectionFactory = (ConnectionFactory) context.lookup("jms
/ConnectionFactory");
Destination queue = (Destination) context.lookup("jms/myQueue");

// Create connection, session, and message producer
Connection connection = connectionFactory.createConnection();
Session session = connection.createSession(false, Session.AUTO_ACKNOWLEDGE);
MessageProducer producer = session.createProducer(queue);

// Create a text message and send it
TextMessage message = session.createTextMessage("Hello, JMS!");
producer.send(message);

// Create a message consumer and register a message listener
MessageConsumer consumer = session.createConsumer(queue);
consumer.setMessageListener(new MessageListener() {
    @Override
    public void onMessage(Message receivedMessage) {
        if (receivedMessage instanceof TextMessage) {
            try {
                String text = ((TextMessage) receivedMessage).getText();
                System.out.println("Received message: " + text);
```

```
            } catch (JMSException e) {
                e.printStackTrace();
            }
        }
    }
});
```

```
// Start the connection
connection.start();
```

```
// Wait for messages to be processed (in a real application, this would be an
ongoing process)
Thread.sleep(5000);
```

```
// Clean up resources
producer.close();
consumer.close();
session.close();
connection.close();
```

Conclusion

The Java Messaging Service (JMS) is a powerful tool for building scalable and asynchronous communication in enterprise applications. It enables applications to exchange data reliably and efficiently, even in distributed and decoupled environments. Whether you need to implement message queues, publish-subscribe systems, or event-driven architectures, JMS provides the necessary features and abstractions to achieve these communication patterns.

Section 16.5: Microservices with Java

Microservices architecture has gained significant popularity in recent years as an approach to building scalable and maintainable software systems. In this section, we'll explore how Java can be used to implement microservices and the key principles behind this architectural style.

What Are Microservices?

Microservices is an architectural style that structures an application as a collection of small, loosely coupled services. Each service is responsible for a specific piece of functionality and can communicate with other services through APIs (typically HTTP or lightweight messaging protocols like Kafka). Microservices promote modularity, independence, and the ability to scale and deploy services independently.

Key Principles of Microservices

1. Service Independence:

Each microservice should be self-contained and responsible for a single business capability. This independence allows teams to develop, deploy, and scale services without affecting others.

2. Decentralized Data Management:

Microservices often have their databases, favoring polyglot persistence. This means using the most suitable database technology for each service's data needs.

3. Communication via APIs:

Services communicate through well-defined APIs. RESTful HTTP or messaging protocols are commonly used for inter-service communication.

4. Infrastructure Automation:

Automation tools like Docker and Kubernetes are frequently used to manage the deployment and scaling of microservices.

5. Continuous Delivery:

Emphasis on continuous integration and continuous delivery (CI/CD) to enable frequent and reliable releases of individual services.

Implementing Microservices in Java

Java is a suitable choice for building microservices due to its strong ecosystem, libraries, and frameworks. Here's a high-level overview of implementing microservices in Java:

1. Spring Boot:

Spring Boot is a popular Java framework for building microservices. It provides a set of tools and conventions for quickly developing production-ready applications. Spring Cloud extends Spring Boot to offer features for building distributed systems, including service discovery, configuration management, and circuit breakers.

2. RESTful APIs:

Microservices are often exposed through RESTful APIs using Spring MVC or JAX-RS (Java API for RESTful Web Services). These APIs allow services to communicate over HTTP.

3. Service Discovery:

Services need a way to locate and communicate with each other. Tools like Netflix Eureka or Kubernetes' service discovery mechanisms can be used.

Docker containers provide a lightweight and consistent environment for running microservices. Docker Compose can be used for managing multi-container applications.

5. *API Gateways:*

An API gateway can aggregate and route requests to various microservices. Spring Cloud Gateway or Netflix Zuul are commonly used for this purpose.

Example Microservices Code

Here's a simplified example of two microservices built with Spring Boot:

Service 1 (Product Service):

```
@RestController
public class ProductController {
    @GetMapping("/products/{id}")
    public Product getProduct(@PathVariable Long id) {
        // Retrieve product details from the database
        return productService.getProductById(id);
    }
}
```

Service 2 (Order Service):

```
@RestController
public class OrderController {
    @GetMapping("/orders/{id}")
    public Order getOrder(@PathVariable Long id) {
        // Retrieve order details from the database
        return orderService.getOrderById(id);
    }
}
```

These services can run independently, and their APIs can be consumed by other services or a frontend application.

Conclusion

Microservices architecture offers a flexible and scalable way to develop complex software systems. Java, with its robust ecosystem and frameworks like Spring Boot, is well-suited for building microservices. By adhering to microservices principles, you can create a system that is easier to develop, maintain, and scale while meeting the demands of modern applications.

Chapter 17: Java for Mobile App Development

Section 17.1: Mobile App Development Options in Java

Mobile app development has become a crucial part of the software industry, given the widespread use of smartphones and tablets. Java offers various options for developing mobile apps, allowing developers to create applications for both Android and iOS platforms. In this section, we will explore these options and their characteristics.

Android App Development with Java

Android, the most popular mobile operating system globally, provides robust support for Java app development. Android app development primarily uses the Java programming language along with the Android Software Development Kit (SDK). Here are some key aspects of Android app development with Java:

1. *Android Studio:* Android app development is typically done using Android Studio, the official integrated development environment (IDE) for Android. It offers a wide range of tools for designing, coding, testing, and debugging Android apps.

2. *Java Programming Language:* Developers can write Android apps using Java, which is a well-established and widely used language. Kotlin, another language, is also supported and increasingly popular for Android development.

3. *XML Layouts:* Android apps use XML files for designing user interfaces. Developers define layouts, views, and widgets in XML files, which are then linked to Java code.

4. *API Access:* Android provides a comprehensive set of APIs for various functionalities, such as UI components, sensors, multimedia, and network operations. Developers can access these APIs to create feature-rich apps.

5. *Emulators and Devices:* Android Studio includes emulators that allow developers to test their apps on virtual Android devices. It also supports debugging on physical Android devices.

6. *Google Play Store:* Once an Android app is developed, it can be published on the Google Play Store, making it accessible to millions of Android users worldwide.

iOS App Development with Java

Developing iOS apps with Java is less common but still possible using some third-party tools and frameworks. Here are a few options for Java-based iOS app development:

1. **RoboVM:** *RoboVM is an open-source platform that allows developers to write iOS apps in Java. It provides a bridge between Java and the native Objective-C runtime, enabling Java code to run on iOS devices.*

2. **LibGDX:** *LibGDX is a popular Java game development framework that supports cross-platform development, including iOS. While it's primarily used for game development, it can be used for other types of apps as well.*

3. **Codename One:** *Codename One is a framework that enables Java developers to write cross-platform mobile apps. It uses Java and provides tools to create native apps for iOS, Android, and other platforms.*

4. **Java-to-iOS Translators:** *Some tools offer Java-to-iOS translation services, converting Java code into Objective-C or Swift code for iOS development.*

It's important to note that while these options allow Java developers to target iOS, they may have limitations compared to using Apple's official development tools and languages (Swift and Objective-C).

Cross-Platform Mobile Development

Another approach for mobile app development is cross-platform development, where a single codebase is used to target multiple platforms, including Android and iOS. Java-based cross-platform frameworks, such as Flutter and Xamarin, enable developers to write code in Java (or C# for Xamarin) and deploy it to both platforms.

In conclusion, Java offers several avenues for mobile app development, with Android being the most prominent platform for Java developers. While Java-based iOS development is possible using third-party tools, it may not provide the same level of integration and native capabilities as Apple's official tools. Cross-platform development frameworks also provide options for Java developers who want to target multiple platforms with a single codebase. The choice of the development approach depends on the specific requirements of the project and the target audience.

Section 17.2: Android App Development with Java

Android app development using Java is a popular choice among developers due to the wide adoption of the Android operating system. In this section, we will delve deeper into the key components and steps involved in developing Android apps with Java.

1. Android Project Structure

When you start an Android app development project in Android Studio, it creates a project structure that includes directories for source code, resources, assets, and more. Here's a brief overview:

- **app/src/main/java:** This directory contains your Java source code files, including the main activity and any additional classes you create.

- **app/src/main/res:** Resources such as XML layout files, images, and strings are stored here. XML files define the layout and appearance of your app's user interface.

- **app/src/main/assets:** If your app needs to include raw asset files (e.g., HTML, JSON, or custom fonts), you can place them here.

2. Activity and Layout

In Android, an "activity" represents a single screen with a user interface. Activities are defined in Java classes and often have associated XML layout files. The layout file specifies how UI elements are arranged on the screen. Here's an example of an activity class and its layout XML:

Java Activity Class (MainActivity.java):

```java
public class MainActivity extends AppCompatActivity {
    @Override
    protected void onCreate(Bundle savedInstanceState) {
        super.onCreate(savedInstanceState);
        setContentView(R.layout.activity_main); // Sets the Layout
    }
}
```

Layout XML (activity_main.xml):

```xml
<?xml version="1.0" encoding="utf-8"?>
<RelativeLayout xmlns:android="http://schemas.android.com/apk/res/android"
    xmlns:app="http://schemas.android.com/apk/res-auto"
    xmlns:tools="http://schemas.android.com/tools"
    android:layout_width="match_parent"
    android:layout_height="match_parent"
    android:padding="16dp"
    tools:context=".MainActivity">

    <TextView
        android:id="@+id/textView"
        android:layout_width="wrap_content"
        android:layout_height="wrap_content"
        android:text="Hello, Android!"
        android:textSize="24sp" />

    <!-- Other UI elements go here -->

</RelativeLayout>
```

3. User Interface and Widgets

Android provides a wide range of UI widgets (e.g., TextViews, Buttons, EditTexts) that you can use to build your app's user interface. You can place these widgets in your XML layout files and interact with them in Java code. Here's an example of setting text for a TextView in Java code:

```java
TextView textView = findViewById(R.id.textView); // Find the TextView by its ID
textView.setText("Hello, Android!"); // Set the text
```

4. Activity Lifecycle

Understanding the Android activity lifecycle is crucial. Activities go through various states (e.g., onCreate, onStart, onResume) as they are created, started, paused, and stopped. Properly managing the lifecycle is essential for ensuring that your app responds correctly to user interactions and system events.

5. Intents and Navigation

Intents are a fundamental concept in Android that enables you to start activities, pass data between activities, and interact with other components of the Android system. You can use explicit intents to launch a specific activity within your app or implicit intents to request an action from another app component, like the camera or a web browser.

6. Permissions

Android apps often require certain permissions to access device features or data. You must declare these permissions in the AndroidManifest.xml file. For example, to access the device's camera, you need to request the CAMERA permission.

7. Gradle Build System

Android Studio uses the Gradle build system to manage dependencies and build your app. You can specify libraries and dependencies in the `build.gradle` files, making it easy to incorporate external code into your project.

8. Testing and Debugging

Android Studio provides robust tools for testing and debugging your apps. You can use emulators or physical devices to test your app during development. The Android Debug Bridge (ADB) allows you to inspect the app's behavior, log messages, and debug issues.

9. Deployment

Once your Android app is complete, you can distribute it through various channels, including the Google Play Store. You need to prepare assets like app icons, screenshots, and descriptions for the store listing. Android Studio assists in generating a signed APK (Android Package) file for publishing.

In summary, Android app development with Java involves creating activities, defining user interfaces, handling the activity lifecycle, managing permissions, and utilizing Gradle for building. Understanding intents, navigation, and testing is also vital. With the right tools and knowledge, you can develop feature-rich Android apps using Java and contribute to the ever-expanding Android ecosystem.

Section 17.3: iOS App Development with Java

While Java is primarily associated with Android app development, there are ways to use Java for iOS app development as well. In this section, we'll explore how to leverage Java to create iOS applications.

1. Java Native Interface (JNI)

The Java Native Interface (JNI) is a crucial technology that enables communication between Java and native code written in other languages like Objective-C, which is commonly used for iOS app development. With JNI, you can bridge the gap between Java and iOS's native frameworks.

Here's a simplified overview of how JNI works in the context of iOS app development:

- **Write Native Code**: You write the core functionality of your iOS app in Objective-C or Swift. This includes user interfaces, interaction with device features, and any other native iOS-specific tasks.

- **Create a JNI Wrapper**: For the parts of your app that you want to implement in Java, you create a JNI wrapper. This wrapper defines native methods that Java can call, acting as a bridge to the native code.

- **Compile and Link**: You compile the JNI wrapper along with your Java code and the native Objective-C/Swift code. The linking process combines these components into a single executable.

- **Execute on iOS**: The resulting executable can run on iOS devices or simulators, allowing your Java code to interact with native iOS functionality.

2. Java on iOS via RoboVM

One popular tool for Java-based iOS development is RoboVM. RoboVM was a free and open-source platform that compiled Java bytecode into native iOS code. However, as of 2017, RoboVM is no longer actively maintained, and its official support has ended.

3. Alternative Approaches

Given the discontinuation of RoboVM, developers seeking to use Java for iOS app development may explore the following alternatives:

- **LibGDX**: While originally designed for game development, LibGDX is a Java-based framework that can be used for general iOS app development. It provides cross-platform support and can be used to target both Android and iOS.

- **Multi-Platform Frameworks**: Some multi-platform frameworks, such as Codename One and Gluon Mobile, enable Java-based development for both Android and iOS. These frameworks typically rely on a combination of Java and native code generation to create platform-specific apps.

- **Cross-Platform Tools**: Cross-platform development tools like Xamarin (C#-based) and Flutter (Dart-based) allow developers to create apps for both Android and iOS while writing the majority of the code in a single language.

It's important to note that while it's possible to use Java for iOS app development, it may not be the most common or straightforward choice. Many iOS developers prefer using Swift or Objective-C, which are native to the platform and offer tight integration with Apple's ecosystem.

In conclusion, while Java can be used for iOS app development through technologies like JNI and tools like RoboVM (though it's no longer actively maintained), there are other alternatives and cross-platform frameworks that may provide more robust and up-to-date solutions for building apps that target both Android and iOS platforms. Developers should carefully evaluate their requirements and choose the most suitable approach for their iOS development projects.

Section 17.4: Cross-Platform Mobile Development

Cross-platform mobile app development has gained immense popularity in recent years due to its ability to create apps that run on multiple platforms with a shared codebase. In this section, we'll explore the concept of cross-platform mobile development and some popular frameworks and tools for achieving it.

1. What is Cross-Platform Mobile Development?

Cross-platform mobile development refers to the practice of writing a single codebase that can be used to build mobile applications for multiple platforms, such as Android and iOS. This approach offers several advantages, including code reusability, reduced development time, and cost savings.

2. Benefits of Cross-Platform Development

Here are some key benefits of cross-platform mobile development:

- **Code Reusability**: Developers can write a significant portion of the app's code once and use it across different platforms, reducing redundancy and saving time.

- **Cost-Efficiency**: Cross-platform development often leads to cost savings, as you don't need separate development teams for each platform.

- **Faster Development**: Rapid development is possible because changes made to the shared codebase are reflected on all platforms simultaneously.

- **Uniform User Experience**: Cross-platform tools aim to provide a consistent user experience across different devices and platforms.

3. Popular Cross-Platform Development Frameworks

a. React Native

React Native, developed by Facebook, is one of the most widely used cross-platform frameworks. It allows developers to build mobile apps using JavaScript and React. React Native provides a rich set of components and a strong developer community.

```javascript
// Example React Native code
import React, { Component } from 'react';
import { View, Text, StyleSheet } from 'react-native';

class MyComponent extends Component {
  render() {
    return (
      <View style={styles.container}>
        <Text>Hello, React Native!</Text>
      </View>
    );
  }
}

const styles = StyleSheet.create({
  container: {
    flex: 1,
    justifyContent: 'center',
    alignItems: 'center',
  },
});

export default MyComponent;
```

b. Flutter

Flutter, developed by Google, uses the Dart programming language and provides a rich set of customizable widgets. It compiles to native ARM code, offering excellent performance.

```dart
// Example Flutter code
import 'package:flutter/material.dart';

void main() {
```

```
  runApp(
    MaterialApp(
      home: Scaffold(
        appBar: AppBar(
          title: Text('Hello, Flutter!'),
        ),
        body: Center(
          child: Text('Hello, Flutter!'),
        ),
      ),
    ),
  );
}
```

c. Xamarin

Xamarin, now a part of Microsoft, allows developers to create cross-platform apps using C#. Xamarin.Forms enables the creation of shared UI components, while Xamarin.iOS and Xamarin.Android allow platform-specific customization.

```
// Example Xamarin.Forms code
using Xamarin.Forms;

public class MyPage : ContentPage
{
    public MyPage()
    {
        Content = new StackLayout
        {
            Children = {
                new Label {
                    Text = "Hello, Xamarin.Forms!",
                    HorizontalOptions = LayoutOptions.CenterAndExpand,
                    VerticalOptions = LayoutOptions.CenterAndExpand
                }
            }
        };
    }
}
```

4. Considerations

While cross-platform development offers numerous advantages, it's essential to consider a few factors:

- **Performance**: Cross-platform apps may have slightly lower performance compared to fully native apps, although this gap has been narrowing with advancements in cross-platform frameworks.

- **UI/UX:** Achieving a consistent and platform-native look and feel can be challenging, but it's possible with careful design and customization.

- **Third-Party Libraries**: Check the availability of third-party libraries and plugins for the cross-platform framework you choose, as this can impact your development.

- **Complex Features**: For apps with highly platform-specific or complex features, you may need to write native code in addition to the shared code.

In conclusion, cross-platform mobile development is a powerful approach for building apps that target multiple platforms efficiently. Frameworks like React Native, Flutter, and Xamarin offer robust solutions, and the choice depends on factors like your team's expertise, project requirements, and desired performance. Careful planning and consideration of the pros and cons will help you make the right choice for your mobile app development project.

Section 17.5: App Distribution and Monetization

Once you've developed a mobile app, the next crucial steps are to distribute it to users and potentially monetize it. In this section, we'll explore strategies for distributing your app and various monetization options available to mobile app developers.

1. App Distribution

a. App Stores

The most common way to distribute mobile apps is through app stores. The two major app stores are:

- **Apple App Store**: For iOS apps.
- **Google Play Store**: For Android apps.

Publishing your app on these platforms gives you access to a vast user base. However, each platform has its review process and guidelines that your app must adhere to.

b. Third-Party App Stores

In addition to the official app stores, there are third-party app stores where you can publish your app. These may provide alternative distribution channels, especially for Android apps. Examples include the Amazon Appstore and Samsung Galaxy Store.

c. Progressive Web Apps (PWAs)

PWAs are web-based applications that can be accessed through web browsers. They offer a cross-platform solution and don't require installation from an app store. PWAs are becoming increasingly popular for certain types of apps.

2. Monetization Options

a. In-App Advertising

In-app advertising involves displaying ads within your app. You can earn revenue through various ad formats, such as banners, interstitials, and rewarded videos. Popular ad networks include Google AdMob, Facebook Audience Network, and Unity Ads.

```
// Example of integrating Google AdMob in an Android app
AdView adView = new AdView(this);
adView.setAdSize(AdSize.BANNER);
adView.setAdUnitId("your-ad-unit-id");
AdRequest adRequest = new AdRequest.Builder().build();
adView.loadAd(adRequest);
```

b. In-App Purchases

Offering in-app purchases allows users to buy digital goods or premium features within your app. This model is often used in freemium apps, where the basic app is free, but users can purchase upgrades.

```
// Example of adding an in-app purchase in an iOS app
let productID = "com.example.myapp.premium"
let product = SKProduct(productIdentifier: productID)

// Present the product and allow the user to make the purchase
```

c. Subscription Models

Subscription-based monetization involves charging users a recurring fee to access premium content or features. This model can provide a steady stream of revenue but requires providing ongoing value to subscribers.

d. Selling Your App

You can choose to sell your app directly to users through app stores. This is a one-time purchase model, and users own the app after buying it.

e. Freemium Model

The freemium model combines free and premium versions of your app. Users can download and use a basic version for free, and you offer premium features or content for a fee.

3. Considerations

When deciding on app distribution and monetization strategies, consider the following:

- **User Experience**: Ensure that ads or monetization methods do not degrade the user experience of your app.

- **Pricing Strategy**: Determine the optimal pricing strategy based on your target audience and competition.

- **App Store Guidelines**: Familiarize yourself with the guidelines of the app stores you plan to publish on to avoid rejection.

- **Marketing and Promotion**: Promote your app through various channels to attract users and potential paying customers.

- **User Feedback**: Listen to user feedback and adapt your monetization strategy based on user preferences and needs.

In conclusion, successfully distributing and monetizing your mobile app requires careful planning and consideration of various factors. By choosing the right distribution channels and monetization methods for your app, you can generate revenue while providing value to your users. Additionally, staying informed about industry trends and user behavior can help you make informed decisions about app distribution and monetization.

Chapter 18: Java and Machine Learning

Section 18.1: Machine Learning Basics

Machine learning (ML) is a branch of artificial intelligence (AI) that focuses on developing algorithms and models that enable computers to learn and make predictions or decisions without being explicitly programmed. ML has gained significant popularity due to its ability to analyze large datasets, discover patterns, and provide insights across various domains. In this section, we'll explore the fundamental concepts and terminology of machine learning.

1. Machine Learning Terminology

a. Dataset

A dataset is a collection of data examples used for training, validation, or testing ML models. It typically consists of input features (attributes) and corresponding target values (labels).

b. Features

Features are the input variables or attributes used by an ML model to make predictions. In a dataset, each data point is described by a set of features.

c. Labels

Labels, also known as target values, are the outcomes or values that an ML model aims to predict. Labels are often used in supervised learning tasks.

d. Model

An ML model is a mathematical representation or algorithm that learns patterns and relationships in the data to make predictions or classifications. Models can be linear, nonlinear, or deep neural networks.

2. Types of Machine Learning

a. Supervised Learning

Supervised learning involves training a model on a labeled dataset, where the model learns to map input features to target labels. Common tasks include regression (predicting continuous values) and classification (predicting categories).

b. Unsupervised Learning

Unsupervised learning aims to discover patterns or structures in data without explicit labels. Clustering and dimensionality reduction are common unsupervised learning tasks.

Reinforcement learning focuses on training agents to make a sequence of decisions to maximize a reward signal. It is widely used in applications like robotics and game playing.

3. Machine Learning Workflow

a. Data Preparation

Data preprocessing involves tasks such as cleaning, normalization, and feature engineering to prepare the dataset for training.

b. Model Selection

Choosing an appropriate ML model architecture and algorithm is crucial. It depends on the problem type, dataset, and desired outcomes.

c. Training

During the training phase, the model learns from the labeled dataset by adjusting its parameters to minimize a predefined loss function.

d. Evaluation

Model performance is evaluated using metrics such as accuracy, precision, recall, and F1-score. Cross-validation helps assess generalization.

e. Deployment

Once trained and evaluated, ML models are deployed to make predictions or decisions in real-world scenarios.

4. Libraries and Frameworks

To implement machine learning in Java, you can use various libraries and frameworks, including:

- **Weka**: Weka is a popular open-source ML library with a graphical user interface for data preprocessing, modeling, and evaluation.

- **WekaDeeplearning4j**: This extension integrates Weka with Deeplearning4j, a deep learning framework.

- **DL4J (Deeplearning4j)**: Deeplearning4j is a powerful deep learning framework for Java that supports various neural network architectures.

- **Apache OpenNLP**: OpenNLP is a library for natural language processing tasks such as text classification and entity recognition.

5. Machine Learning Applications

Machine learning finds applications in numerous fields, including:

- **Natural Language Processing (NLP)**: Sentiment analysis, chatbots, and language translation.

- **Computer Vision**: Object detection, image classification, and facial recognition.

- **Healthcare**: Disease diagnosis, drug discovery, and personalized medicine.

- **Finance**: Fraud detection, stock market prediction, and credit scoring.

- **Recommendation Systems**: Personalized content recommendations in e-commerce and entertainment.

In conclusion, machine learning is a powerful technology that enables computers to learn from data and make intelligent predictions. Understanding the core concepts and terminology is essential for anyone interested in applying ML to solve real-world problems. In the following sections, we will delve deeper into ML libraries, frameworks, and practical implementations in Java.

Section 18.2: Libraries and Frameworks for ML in Java

In the realm of machine learning (ML) and artificial intelligence (AI), Java offers a variety of libraries and frameworks to facilitate the development of ML models and applications. These libraries provide the necessary tools and abstractions to streamline tasks such as data preprocessing, model training, and evaluation. In this section, we will explore some of the most notable libraries and frameworks for ML in Java.

1. Deeplearning4j (DL4J)

Deeplearning4j is a versatile deep learning framework specifically designed for Java. It enables the development of various neural network architectures, including convolutional neural networks (CNNs) and recurrent neural networks (RNNs). DL4J supports both CPU and GPU acceleration, making it suitable for training complex models on large datasets.

Example DL4J code for building a simple neural network:

```
import org.deeplearning4j.nn.api.OptimizationAlgorithm;
import org.deeplearning4j.nn.conf.MultiLayerConfiguration;
import org.deeplearning4j.nn.conf.NeuralNetConfiguration;
import org.deeplearning4j.nn.conf.layers.DenseLayer;
import org.deeplearning4j.nn.conf.layers.OutputLayer;
import org.deeplearning4j.nn.multilayer.MultiLayerNetwork;
import org.deeplearning4j.nn.weights.WeightInit;
import org.nd4j.linalg.activations.Activation;
import org.nd4j.linalg.learning.config.Adam;
import org.nd4j.linalg.lossfunctions.LossFunctions;

// Define a simple feedforward neural network
MultiLayerConfiguration configuration = new NeuralNetConfiguration.Builder()
```

```
        .seed(123)
        .optimizationAlgo(OptimizationAlgorithm.STOCHASTIC_GRADIENT_DESCENT)
        .weightInit(WeightInit.XAVIER)
        .updater(new Adam(0.001))
        .list()
        .layer(new DenseLayer.Builder()
            .nIn(784)   // Input size
            .nOut(128)  // Output size
            .activation(Activation.RELU)
            .build())
        .layer(new OutputLayer.Builder(LossFunctions.LossFunction.NEGATIVELOGLIKE
LIHOOD)
            .nIn(128)
            .nOut(10)   // Output classes
            .activation(Activation.SOFTMAX)
            .build())
        .build();

// Create and configure the neural network
MultiLayerNetwork neuralNetwork = new MultiLayerNetwork(configuration);
neuralNetwork.init();
```

2. Weka

Weka (Waikato Environment for Knowledge Analysis) is a popular open-source machine learning library written in Java. It provides a graphical user interface (GUI) for performing various ML tasks, making it accessible to both beginners and experts. Weka offers a wide range of algorithms for classification, regression, clustering, and data preprocessing.

Example Weka code for loading a dataset and training a classifier:

```
import weka.classifiers.Classifier;
import weka.classifiers.Evaluation;
import weka.classifiers.functions.Logistic;
import weka.core.Instances;
import weka.core.converters.ConverterUtils.DataSource;

// Load a dataset from a file
DataSource source = new DataSource("iris.arff");
Instances dataset = source.getDataSet();

// Set the class attribute (target variable)
dataset.setClassIndex(dataset.numAttributes() - 1);

// Create a logistic regression classifier
Classifier classifier = new Logistic();

// Train the classifier on the dataset
classifier.buildClassifier(dataset);
```

```
// Evaluate the classifier using cross-validation
Evaluation evaluation = new Evaluation(dataset);
evaluation.crossValidateModel(classifier, dataset, 10, new Random(1));

// Print evaluation results
System.out.println(evaluation.toSummaryString());
```

3. Apache OpenNLP

Apache OpenNLP is a natural language processing (NLP) library for Java. While it specializes in tasks like text classification, entity recognition, and parsing, it can be used in conjunction with other ML libraries to create NLP-driven ML models.

Example OpenNLP code for text classification:

```
import opennlp.tools.doccat.DoccatModel;
import opennlp.tools.doccat.DocumentCategorizerME;
import opennlp.tools.doccat.DocumentSample;
import opennlp.tools.doccat.DocumentSampleStream;
import opennlp.tools.util.ObjectStream;
import opennlp.tools.util.PlainTextByLineStream;
import opennlp.tools.util.TrainingParameters;

import java.io.*;
import java.util.ArrayList;
import java.util.List;

// Prepare training data (documents with categories)
List<DocumentSample> trainingData = new ArrayList<>();
trainingData.add(new DocumentSample("I like programming.", "programming"));
trainingData.add(new DocumentSample("The cat is on the mat.", "other"));

// Train a text classifier model
ObjectStream<DocumentSample> stream = new DocumentSampleStream(trainingData);
DoccatModel model = DocumentCategorizerME.train("en", stream, TrainingParamet
ers.defaultParams());

// Create a DocumentCategorizerME instance
DocumentCategorizerME categorizer = new DocumentCategorizerME(model);

// Classify a document
String document = "I
```

##
Section 18.3: Building ML Models with Java

Building machine learning (ML) models in Java involves the process of selecting the right algorithms, preparing and cleaning the data, training the models, and evaluating their performance. Java offers a variety of libraries and tools that streamline these tasks and facilitate the development of ML models.

In this section, we will explore the process of building ML models in Java.

1. Data Preprocessing

Before building an ML model, it's essential to preprocess the data. This involves tasks such as data cleaning, handling missing values, encoding categorical variables, and scaling features. Libraries like Apache Commons Math and Weka provide utilities for data preprocessing.

Example data preprocessing code using Apache Commons Math:

```java
import org.apache.commons.math3.analysis.function.Sigmoid;
import org.apache.commons.math3.linear.Array2DRowRealMatrix;
import org.apache.commons.math3.linear.RealMatrix;
import org.apache.commons.math3.linear.RealVector;
import org.apache.commons.math3.stat.correlation.PearsonsCorrelation;

// Create a matrix of data (features)
double[][] data = {{1.2, 2.4, 3.6}, {2.5, 3.0, 4.2}, {3.3, 1.8, 2.0}};
RealMatrix matrix = new Array2DRowRealMatrix(data);

// Calculate the mean and standard deviation of each column
RealVector mean = matrix.getRowVector(0);   // Replace with your mean values
RealVector stdDev = matrix.getRowVector(1);   // Replace with your std deviation values

// Standardize the data
matrix = matrix.subtract(mean).scalarMultiply(1.0 / stdDev);

// Calculate the correlation matrix
PearsonsCorrelation correlation = new PearsonsCorrelation(matrix);
RealMatrix correlationMatrix = correlation.getCorrelationMatrix();
```

2. Model Selection

Choosing the right ML algorithm for your problem is crucial. Java libraries like Deeplearning4j, Weka, and Apache OpenNLP provide various algorithms for classification, regression, clustering, and more. The choice depends on the nature of your data and the specific task you want to solve.

3. Model Training

Once you've selected an algorithm, you need to train the ML model using your dataset. This involves splitting the data into training and testing sets, feeding it to the algorithm, and adjusting the model's parameters. Here's an example of training a decision tree classifier using Weka:

```java
import weka.classifiers.Classifier;
import weka.classifiers.trees.J48;
import weka.core.Instances;
import weka.core.converters.ConverterUtils.DataSource;
import weka.core.converters.ArffLoader;

// Load a dataset from a file
DataSource source = new DataSource("iris.arff");
Instances dataset = source.getDataSet();
dataset.setClassIndex(dataset.numAttributes() - 1);

// Create a decision tree classifier
Classifier classifier = new J48();

// Train the classifier on the dataset
classifier.buildClassifier(dataset);
```

4. Model Evaluation

After training, it's essential to evaluate the model's performance. Metrics like accuracy, precision, recall, and F1-score can help assess how well the model generalizes to unseen data. Java libraries provide tools for conducting cross-validation and calculating these metrics.

Example code to evaluate a classifier using Weka:

```java
import weka.classifiers.Evaluation;
import weka.core.Instances;
import weka.core.converters.ConverterUtils.DataSource;

// Load a dataset from a file
DataSource source = new DataSource("iris.arff");
Instances dataset = source.getDataSet();
dataset.setClassIndex(dataset.numAttributes() - 1);

// Create a classifier (already trained on the training data)

// Evaluate the classifier using cross-validation
Evaluation evaluation = new Evaluation(dataset);
evaluation.crossValidateModel(classifier, dataset, 10, new Random(1));

// Print evaluation results
System.out.println(evaluation.toSummaryString());
```

5. Hyperparameter Tuning and Optimization

To improve model performance, you can fine-tune hyperparameters and optimize algorithms. Libraries like Deeplearning4j and Weka provide options for grid search and automatic hyperparameter tuning.

Building ML models in Java involves a combination of data preprocessing, algorithm selection, training, evaluation, and optimization. The choice of libraries and tools depends on the specific ML tasks you aim to tackle and the complexity of your data.

Remember that successful ML model development often requires a deep understanding of both the domain and the ML techniques you're employing. Experimentation, iteration, and continuous learning are key to achieving the best results.

Section 18.4: Deployment of ML Models

Once you've trained a machine learning (ML) model in Java, the next step is to deploy it for use in production environments. Deployment involves making the model accessible for predictions, either through web services, mobile applications, or other interfaces. In this section, we'll explore the deployment of ML models in Java.

1. Exporting Models

Before deployment, you need to export your trained ML model into a format that can be used by Java applications. Common formats include PMML (Predictive Model Markup Language), serialized Java objects, or model-specific formats supported by ML libraries like Deeplearning4j.

Example code to serialize and save a trained model using Java's built-in serialization:

```java
import java.io.*;

// Assume 'model' is your trained ML model
try (ObjectOutputStream oos = new ObjectOutputStream(new FileOutputStream("mo
del.ser"))) {
    oos.writeObject(model);
}
```

2. Creating a Service

To make ML predictions accessible, you can create a web service using Java frameworks like Spring Boot or Apache CXF. These frameworks provide the infrastructure to expose your model through RESTful APIs.

Example code to create a RESTful web service using Spring Boot:

```java
import org.springframework.boot.SpringApplication;
import org.springframework.boot.autoconfigure.SpringBootApplication;
import org.springframework.web.bind.annotation.PostMapping;
import org.springframework.web.bind.annotation.RequestBody;
import org.springframework.web.bind.annotation.RestController;

@SpringBootApplication
public class MLServiceApplication {
```

```java
    public static void main(String[] args) {
        SpringApplication.run(MLServiceApplication.class, args);
    }
}

@RestController
public class MLController {
    @PostMapping("/predict")
    public String predict(@RequestBody String input) {
        // Deserialize the model (similar to the previous section)
        // Use the model to make predictions
        // Return the predictions as JSON or other suitable format
        return "Predicted result: ...";
    }
}
```

3. Containerization

Containerization using technologies like Docker and Kubernetes simplifies the deployment of ML models. You can package your Java application, including the model and the web service, into a Docker container and deploy it to a Kubernetes cluster for scalability and management.

4. Real-Time and Batch Processing

Depending on your use case, ML models can be deployed for real-time or batch processing. Real-time processing involves handling predictions as they come in, while batch processing deals with large datasets or scheduled jobs. Java offers libraries like Apache Kafka and Apache Flink for real-time data streaming and batch processing.

5. Monitoring and Scaling

Monitoring the deployed ML model's performance is critical. Java-based tools like Prometheus and Grafana can help you collect and visualize metrics. Scaling can be achieved by deploying multiple instances of your service behind a load balancer or by using cloud-based solutions like AWS Lambda or Google Cloud Functions.

6. Security and Compliance

Ensure that your deployed ML service adheres to security best practices. Implement authentication, authorization, and encryption to protect data and models. If your application deals with sensitive data, consider compliance with regulations like GDPR or HIPAA.

Deployment of ML models in Java involves a combination of exporting models, creating services, containerization, real-time or batch processing, monitoring, scaling, and ensuring security and compliance. The choice of deployment approach depends on your specific use case and requirements. It's essential to maintain and update deployed models as new data becomes available and to continuously monitor their performance for optimal results.

Section 18.5: Real-World ML Applications

In this section, we'll delve into real-world applications of machine learning (ML) in Java. Machine learning has a wide range of applications across various industries, and Java plays a significant role in implementing and deploying ML solutions. Here are some practical examples of ML applications in the real world:

1. E-commerce Recommendations

E-commerce platforms like Amazon and Netflix use ML algorithms to analyze user behavior and make personalized product or content recommendations. Java is commonly used to implement these recommendation systems, which rely on collaborative filtering and content-based filtering techniques.

2. Fraud Detection

Financial institutions employ ML models to detect fraudulent activities, such as credit card fraud or unauthorized access to accounts. These models analyze transaction data and user behavior patterns. Java is often used to build and deploy these fraud detection systems securely.

3. Healthcare Diagnostics

ML models in Java can assist medical professionals in diagnosing diseases based on medical records, images, and patient data. For instance, image recognition models can identify anomalies in medical images, while natural language processing (NLP) models can extract insights from clinical notes.

4. Autonomous Vehicles

Java is used in developing software for autonomous vehicles, where ML models are essential for tasks like object detection, lane following, and decision-making. ML helps vehicles perceive and navigate their environment safely.

5. Customer Support Chatbots

Many businesses employ chatbots powered by ML and NLP to handle customer inquiries and support requests. Java-based chatbots can understand and respond to user queries effectively.

6. Energy Consumption Optimization

ML models can analyze energy consumption patterns in buildings and industrial facilities. Java is used to build software that optimizes energy usage by adjusting HVAC systems, lighting, and other parameters based on historical data.

7. Natural Language Processing (NLP)

Java-based NLP models can be applied in sentiment analysis, language translation, and text summarization. These models enable applications to understand and generate human-like text.

8. Supply Chain Optimization

ML algorithms can optimize supply chain operations by predicting demand, managing inventory, and optimizing transportation routes. Java plays a role in creating these intelligent supply chain solutions.

9. Recommendation Engines for Content

Media streaming services like Spotify and YouTube employ ML models to recommend music and videos to users. Java is used for implementing recommendation algorithms and personalization.

10. Environmental Monitoring

ML models in Java can analyze environmental data, such as weather patterns, air quality, and satellite imagery. This information is vital for climate modeling, disaster prediction, and resource management.

11. Cybersecurity

Java is used in building security applications that leverage ML to detect and respond to cyber threats. ML models can identify abnormal network behavior and potential security breaches.

12. Retail Inventory Management

Retailers use ML to optimize inventory levels, reducing costs and minimizing out-of-stock situations. Java-based solutions can handle large-scale inventory data and make real-time decisions.

These examples demonstrate the versatility of ML in solving real-world problems across diverse domains. Java's robustness, scalability, and the availability of ML libraries make it a valuable tool for implementing and deploying ML solutions in various industries and applications. As ML continues to advance, its impact on industries and society is likely to grow, with Java playing a significant role in shaping the future of machine learning applications.

Chapter 19: Java for Game Development

Section 19.1: Game Development Frameworks in Java

In this section, we'll explore the world of game development using Java. Game development is a fascinating field that combines creativity, programming skills, and a deep understanding of user engagement. Java is a versatile language for developing games, and it offers various game development frameworks and libraries to streamline the process.

Why Choose Java for Game Development?

Before we dive into game development frameworks, let's briefly discuss why Java is a popular choice for creating games:

- **Platform Independence:** Java's "write once, run anywhere" mantra makes it suitable for cross-platform game development. Games developed in Java can run on Windows, macOS, Linux, and even Android devices.

- **Strong Ecosystem:** Java has a rich ecosystem of libraries and tools that aid game development, including graphics libraries, physics engines, and sound libraries.

- **Performance:** Modern Java versions offer excellent performance, and with the right optimization techniques, Java games can be fast and responsive.

- **Community and Resources:** Java has a vibrant developer community, which means you can find ample resources, tutorials, and support for your game development journey.

Popular Game Development Frameworks in Java

Let's explore some of the widely used game development frameworks and libraries available in the Java ecosystem:

1. LibGDX

LibGDX

LibGDX is a powerful and highly extensible open-source framework for game development in Java. It provides essential features such as 2D and 3D rendering, input handling, physics simulations, and cross-platform deployment. LibGDX has gained popularity for developing both 2D and 3D games, and it has a large community contributing to its growth.

2. jMonkeyEngine

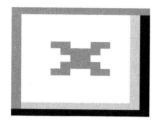

jMonkeyEngine

jMonkeyEngine is a robust 3D game engine written in Java. It offers advanced features like scene graphs, physics simulations, and support for shaders. jMonkeyEngine is suitable for developers looking to create 3D games and simulations with Java.

3. Slick2D

Slick2D is a simple and easy-to-use 2D game library for Java. It provides features like sprite rendering, input handling, and sound support. While it may not have as many advanced features as LibGDX or jMonkeyEngine, Slick2D is an excellent choice for beginners and small-scale 2D game projects.

4. LWJGL (Lightweight Java Game Library)

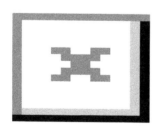

LWJGL

LWJGL is a low-level Java library that enables access to native APIs for graphics, audio, and input. While it's not a game engine itself, LWJGL is used by many game developers to create custom game engines tailored to their specific needs. It provides the flexibility to optimize performance-critical aspects of game development.

5. PlayN

PlayN is an open-source game development framework that allows you to write games in Java and deploy them across different platforms, including web, desktop, and mobile. It abstracts platform-specific details, making cross-platform development more accessible.

Choosing the Right Framework

The choice of a game development framework largely depends on your project's requirements, your familiarity with the framework, and the type of game you intend to create. Each framework mentioned above has its strengths and weaknesses, so it's essential to evaluate them based on your specific needs.

In the subsequent sections of this chapter, we'll explore various aspects of game development in Java, including graphics rendering, user input handling, physics simulations, and game design patterns. Whether you're a beginner looking to create your first game or an experienced developer seeking to expand your game development skills, this chapter will provide valuable insights into the world of game development using Java.

Section 19.2: Game Physics and Animation

In the realm of game development, physics and animation play pivotal roles in creating realistic and engaging gaming experiences. This section delves into the importance of game physics and animation, how they impact gameplay, and the tools and techniques available for implementing them in Java-based game projects.

The Significance of Game Physics

Game physics is the simulation of real-world physical behaviors within a game environment. It encompasses a wide range of phenomena, including gravity, collision detection, object interactions, and motion dynamics. Implementing realistic physics can greatly enhance the immersion and authenticity of a game.

In Java game development, there are several libraries and engines that provide physics simulations. One notable option is the physics engine integrated into the LibGDX framework, which offers features like rigid body physics, collision detection, and joint constraints. By utilizing these tools, developers can create games with lifelike physics interactions.

Animation in Games

Animation is another critical aspect of game development that brings characters, objects, and environments to life. It involves creating the illusion of motion by rapidly displaying a sequence of images or altering the properties of game objects over time. Animation adds visual appeal and responsiveness to games.

For 2D game development in Java, tools like LibGDX provide powerful animation capabilities. Developers can create sprite sheets, define animation sequences, and control the playback of animations with ease. Additionally, tweening libraries, such as Universal Tween Engine, simplify the process of animating properties like position, scale, and opacity.

In the realm of 3D game development, libraries like jMonkeyEngine offer advanced animation systems that support skeletal animation, keyframe animation, and blending between animations. These features enable the creation of lifelike character animations and dynamic object movements.

Implementing Game Physics

Implementing game physics in Java involves defining the behavior of game objects and simulating their interactions. This typically requires:

1. **Collision Detection:** Detecting when game objects intersect with each other or with the game world. Various algorithms, such as bounding boxes and polygons, are used for collision detection.

2. **Rigid Body Dynamics:** Simulating the motion and behavior of objects with mass, inertia, and forces applied to them. Physics engines handle this aspect and calculate positions and velocities.

3. **Collision Response:** Defining how objects react when collisions occur, including bouncing, sliding, or destruction. This aspect adds realism to games.

4. **Gravity and Forces:** Applying forces like gravity, friction, and user input to influence object movement. These forces contribute to dynamic gameplay.

Developers often need to fine-tune these physics parameters to strike a balance between realism and enjoyable gameplay.

Creating Game Animation

To create animations in Java games, developers typically follow these steps:

1. **Asset Preparation:** Design and create individual frames of animation, which are often organized into sprite sheets or sequences of images.

2. **Loading Assets:** Load animation assets into the game, either at startup or dynamically as needed.

3. **Defining Animation Sequences:** Define animation sequences by specifying which frames to play in what order and at what speed.

4. **Controlling Animation:** Implement logic to control when animations should start, stop, or change based on in-game events or user input.

5. **Rendering:** During the game's rendering loop, display the appropriate frame of the animation on the screen.

For 3D games, character animations often involve skeletal rigs and keyframes. Artists create animations in software like Blender or Maya, and game developers import these animations into the game engine for playback.

Conclusion

Game physics and animation are vital components of the game development process. They contribute to the realism, interactivity, and overall quality of the gaming experience. Whether you're creating a 2D platformer or a 3D action-adventure game in Java, understanding and implementing physics and animation techniques will help you craft engaging and immersive gameplay.

Section 19.3: Game Design Patterns

Game design patterns are reusable solutions to common problems that arise during game development. These patterns provide a structured approach to designing and implementing game systems, making it easier to create high-quality games. In this section, we'll explore some essential game design patterns and how they can be applied in Java game development.

The Role of Design Patterns

Design patterns are crucial in game development because they help manage complexity, promote code reusability, and improve maintainability. By following established patterns, game developers can focus on creating unique gameplay experiences rather than reinventing the wheel for each game component.

Singleton Pattern

The Singleton pattern ensures that a class has only one instance and provides a global point of access to that instance. This pattern is useful for managing game systems like the game engine, audio manager, or resource loader, where having multiple instances can lead to inefficiencies or inconsistent behavior.

In Java, the Singleton pattern can be implemented using a private constructor, a private static instance variable, and a public static method to access the instance. Here's a simple example:

```java
public class GameManager {
    private static GameManager instance;

    private GameManager() {
        // Private constructor to prevent external instantiation.
    }

    public static GameManager getInstance() {
        if (instance == null) {
            instance = new GameManager();
        }
        return instance;
    }

    // Other game-related methods and properties.
}
```

Observer Pattern

The Observer pattern is used to implement a one-to-many dependency between objects, where one object (the subject) maintains a list of dependents (observers) that are notified of any state changes. In game development, this pattern is valuable for handling events, notifications, and updates.

In Java, you can implement the Observer pattern using built-in classes like `java.util.Observable` and `java.util.Observer`. Alternatively, you can create custom observer interfaces and classes tailored to your game's needs.

```java
import java.util.Observable;
import java.util.Observer;

public class Player implements Observer {
    // Other player-related properties and methods.

    @Override
    public void update(Observable observable, Object arg) {
        if (observable instanceof GameEventSubject) {
            GameEventSubject eventSubject = (GameEventSubject) observable;
            // Handle game events here.
        }
    }
}
```

Factory Pattern

The Factory pattern is used to create objects without specifying the exact class of object that will be created. In game development, this pattern is beneficial for generating game entities, such as enemies, power-ups, or projectiles, without exposing the concrete implementation details.

Here's a simplified example of a game entity factory in Java:

```java
public abstract class EntityFactory {
    public abstract Entity createEntity();
}

public class EnemyFactory extends EntityFactory {
    @Override
    public Entity createEntity() {
        // Create and configure an enemy object.
        return new Enemy();
    }
}

public class PowerUpFactory extends EntityFactory {
    @Override
    public Entity createEntity() {
        // Create and configure a power-up object.
        return new PowerUp();
    }
}
```

Conclusion

These are just a few examples of game design patterns that can significantly improve the structure and maintainability of your Java game projects. By incorporating these patterns into your game development workflow, you can streamline development, reduce bugs, and create more extensible and scalable games. Game design patterns are powerful tools that help you focus on what makes your game unique while benefiting from the collective wisdom of the game development community.

Section 19.4: Multiplayer Game Development

Multiplayer game development is an exciting and challenging endeavor that allows players to interact with each other in real-time, creating a dynamic and engaging gaming experience. In this section, we'll explore the key concepts and techniques involved in developing multiplayer games using Java.

Client-Server Architecture

Most multiplayer games follow a client-server architecture, where one machine (the server) hosts the game world and manages the game's state, while multiple client machines connect to the server to participate in the game. The server acts as the central authority, ensuring that game rules are followed and synchronizing the state across all clients.

Here's a simplified overview of the client-server interaction:

1. Clients connect to the server.

2. Clients send input commands to the server (e.g., move, shoot).
3. The server processes commands, updates the game state, and sends updates to all connected clients.
4. Clients receive updates from the server and render the game accordingly.

Networking in Java

Java provides libraries and APIs for implementing networking in multiplayer games. The java.net package offers classes for working with sockets, which are essential for establishing network connections between clients and servers.

For example, creating a server socket in Java can be done as follows:

```java
import java.io.IOException;
import java.net.ServerSocket;
import java.net.Socket;

public class GameServer {
    public static void main(String[] args) {
        int port = 12345;

        try {
            ServerSocket serverSocket = new ServerSocket(port);
            System.out.println("Server is running on port " + port);

            while (true) {
                Socket clientSocket = serverSocket.accept();
                // Handle client connection in a separate thread or class.
            }
        } catch (IOException e) {
            e.printStackTrace();
        }
    }
}
```

Synchronization and Latency

One of the challenges in multiplayer game development is dealing with network latency and ensuring that all players see a consistent game state. This involves predicting player actions on the client side, sending them to the server, and reconciling any discrepancies.

Common techniques for handling synchronization and latency include:

- Dead reckoning: Predicting the positions of objects based on their last known state and velocity.
- Interpolation: Smoothing out the movement of objects by interpolating between known positions.
- Server reconciliation: Resolving differences between client and server states by applying server-authoritative updates.

Game Lobby and Matchmaking

Multiplayer games often include features like game lobbies and matchmaking systems to help players find opponents and create balanced matches. These systems use algorithms to group players with similar skill levels and preferences.

Implementing a game lobby and matchmaking system involves creating user interfaces, managing player sessions, and ensuring a fair and enjoyable multiplayer experience.

Security and Cheating Prevention

Security is a critical aspect of multiplayer game development. Games must prevent cheating, such as aimbots or wallhacks, to maintain a fair gaming environment. Techniques like server-side validation, encryption, and anti-cheat software are commonly used to address security concerns.

Developers also need to consider data privacy and protect user information when implementing multiplayer features that involve user accounts, chat systems, or social interactions.

Conclusion

Multiplayer game development in Java is an exciting journey that requires a deep understanding of networking, synchronization, and user experience. By following best practices and leveraging the Java networking libraries, you can create engaging and competitive multiplayer games that provide players with hours of fun and excitement.

Section 19.5: Publishing and Marketing Games

Publishing and marketing games are crucial steps in bringing your game to a wider audience and ensuring its success in a competitive market. In this section, we'll explore the key strategies and considerations for effectively publishing and marketing your Java games.

Preparing for Launch

Before launching your game, it's essential to ensure that it's polished and thoroughly tested. This includes fixing any bugs, optimizing performance, and incorporating player feedback from testing phases. Create a compelling gameplay trailer and captivating screenshots that showcase your game's unique features.

Choosing a Distribution Platform

Selecting the right distribution platform is a pivotal decision. Some popular options for publishing Java games include:

1. **Steam**: Steam is a well-known platform for PC gaming. To publish on Steam, you'll need to go through their Greenlight or Steam Direct process.

2. **Google Play Store**: If you're developing an Android game, the Google Play Store is a primary distribution channel for mobile games.

3. **Apple App Store**: For iOS games, the Apple App Store is the primary platform for distribution.

4. **Itch.io**: Itch.io is an indie-friendly platform that allows you to self-publish your games.

5. **Indie Game Stores**: Some independent game stores specialize in promoting and selling indie games, providing exposure to a niche audience.

6. **Your Website**: Self-publishing on your website allows you to retain more control over distribution and revenue, but it may require more marketing effort.

Marketing Strategies

Effective marketing is essential to make your game stand out in a crowded market. Consider the following marketing strategies:

- **Create a Website**: Develop a professional website for your game with information, screenshots, videos, and a blog to keep players engaged.

- **Social Media**: Establish a presence on social media platforms like Twitter, Facebook, and Instagram. Share development updates, engage with your audience, and run targeted ads.

- **Press Releases**: Write and distribute press releases to gaming news websites and influencers to generate buzz about your game.

- **Game Demos**: Offer a free demo or trial version of your game to allow players to experience it before purchase.

- **Community Building**: Build a community around your game through forums, Discord servers, or Reddit. Engage with players, listen to feedback, and provide support.

- **Email Marketing**: Collect email addresses from interested players and send them updates, exclusive content, and release announcements.

- **Influencer Marketing**: Collaborate with YouTubers, Twitch streamers, and other influencers to showcase your game to their audiences.

- **Game Jams and Events**: Participate in game jams, conventions, and gaming events to network with industry professionals and fellow developers.

Monetization Strategies

Consider how you'll monetize your game. Common monetization models include:

- **Paid Games**: Charging an upfront fee for the game.

- **Free-to-Play (F2P)**: Offering the game for free and generating revenue through in-app purchases or ads.
- **Subscription**: Providing access to the game through a monthly or yearly subscription.
- **DLCs and Expansions**: Releasing additional content or expansions for a fee.

Ensure that your chosen monetization strategy aligns with your target audience and the nature of your game.

Post-Launch Support

After launching your game, continue to support it with updates, bug fixes, and additional content. Engage with the player community and respond to their feedback promptly. Positive post-launch support can lead to increased player loyalty and word-of-mouth recommendations.

In conclusion, the success of your Java game not only depends on its quality but also on effective publishing and marketing strategies. By carefully planning your launch, choosing the right distribution platform, and implementing a robust marketing campaign, you can increase your game's visibility and attract a loyal player base. Consistent post-launch support and monetization strategies are equally important to sustain your game's success in the long run.

Chapter 20: Future Trends in Java

Section 20.1: Java for Quantum Computing

Quantum computing is an emerging field that holds the promise of solving complex problems exponentially faster than classical computers. While Java has primarily been associated with traditional computing, it is also making strides in quantum computing. In this section, we'll explore the role of Java in the world of quantum computing and its potential applications.

Understanding Quantum Computing

Quantum computing leverages the principles of quantum mechanics to perform calculations. Unlike classical bits, quantum bits or qubits can exist in multiple states simultaneously, enabling quantum computers to explore many solutions at once. This property makes quantum computers exceptionally powerful for certain types of problems, such as factorization, optimization, and simulating quantum systems.

Quantum Programming Languages

Quantum programming languages are essential for writing quantum algorithms and leveraging quantum hardware. While languages like Qiskit (for IBM's quantum devices) and Cirq (for Google's quantum devices) are prevalent, there is also a growing interest in using Java for quantum programming.

Quantum Libraries in Java

Several Java libraries and frameworks are emerging to facilitate quantum computing:

- **Quantum Development Kit (QDK)**: Developed by Microsoft, the QDK includes a Q# quantum programming language and libraries. It offers interoperability with Java through the Java Native Interface (JNI).

- **JQuantum**: JQuantum is an open-source Java library that provides a high-level interface to quantum hardware and simulators. It simplifies quantum programming in Java and supports various quantum processors.

- **Quantum Inspire**: Quantum Inspire is a platform that allows Java developers to access quantum simulators and hardware via RESTful APIs.

Quantum Computing Applications in Java

Java's role in quantum computing is not limited to developing quantum algorithms. It also extends to building classical components of hybrid quantum-classical systems. Here are some potential applications:

- **Quantum Machine Learning**: Java can be used to develop classical machine learning components that work in tandem with quantum algorithms to solve complex problems.

- **Cryptography**: Quantum computing threatens classical cryptography algorithms. Java can help implement and integrate post-quantum cryptography solutions.

- **Quantum Simulations**: Java can be used to build simulations and tools for understanding quantum systems, even before practical quantum hardware is widely available.

- **Hybrid Quantum Systems**: Java can be the bridge between classical and quantum components in hybrid quantum-classical systems.

Challenges and Opportunities

While Java's entry into quantum computing is exciting, there are challenges to overcome. Quantum programming is fundamentally different from classical programming, and developers must learn new concepts. Additionally, quantum hardware is still in its infancy, and widespread adoption will take time.

However, Java's strengths in portability, community support, and robust libraries make it a viable choice for quantum computing development. As quantum technologies advance, Java's role is likely to grow, enabling developers to harness the potential of quantum computing for solving complex real-world problems.

Section 20.2: Java for Augmented and Virtual Reality

Augmented Reality (AR) and Virtual Reality (VR) are transformative technologies that blend the digital and physical worlds, offering immersive and interactive experiences. Java, with its robust ecosystem and cross-platform capabilities, is increasingly being used for AR and VR development. In this section, we'll explore how Java is playing a role in these cutting-edge fields.

Augmented Reality with Java

Java is well-suited for creating AR applications due to its portability and extensive libraries. Here's how Java is involved in AR development:

1. **ARCore and ARKit Support**: Java can be used to develop Android AR apps that leverage ARCore and iOS AR apps that use ARKit. Developers can use Android Studio (Java-based) or Swift (for iOS) to build AR applications.

2. **Cross-Platform AR**: Java's cross-platform capabilities make it possible to write AR apps that work on multiple platforms. Libraries like LibGDX, which have Java bindings, can be used for cross-platform AR game development.

3. **Computer Vision**: Java's robust support for computer vision libraries, such as OpenCV, can be used to create AR applications that recognize and interact with the physical world.

Virtual Reality with Java

Java is also gaining traction in the VR space, allowing developers to create immersive virtual environments:

1. **Game Development**: Java game engines like jMonkeyEngine and LibGDX can be used to build VR games. These engines provide tools for creating 3D worlds and handling user interactions.

2. **Simulations**: VR is not limited to gaming. Java is used in fields like education and training to develop VR simulations for training and education purposes.

3. **WebVR**: Java can be used to create VR experiences for the web. WebVR libraries and frameworks, combined with Java for web development, enable VR content accessible through web browsers.

Challenges and Opportunities

While Java has made strides in AR and VR development, challenges remain:

- **Performance**: VR demands high performance to provide a smooth and immersive experience. Developers need to optimize their Java code for performance.

- **Hardware Compatibility**: AR and VR applications often rely on specialized hardware like headsets and controllers. Ensuring compatibility with various devices can be challenging.

- **Learning Curve**: Developing for AR and VR requires a good understanding of 3D graphics, physics, and user interaction. Developers may need to acquire new skills.

However, Java's cross-platform capabilities and vast developer community make it a valuable choice for AR and VR development. As these technologies continue to evolve and gain popularity, Java is likely to play an even more significant role in shaping the future of augmented and virtual reality experiences.

Section 20.3: Java in the World of Blockchain

Blockchain technology has gained widespread attention and application in various industries, and Java is becoming increasingly relevant in this space. In this section, we'll explore how Java is being used for blockchain development, the advantages it brings, and some of the challenges it faces.

Java's portability, security features, and extensive libraries make it a suitable choice for blockchain development. Here are some key areas where Java is making an impact in the blockchain world:

1. **Smart Contracts**: Ethereum, one of the most popular blockchain platforms, supports the development of smart contracts using a language called Solidity. However, there are efforts to bring Java compatibility to Ethereum, allowing developers to write smart contracts in Java. This provides Java developers with access to the Ethereum ecosystem.

2. **Blockchain Integration**: Java can be used to integrate blockchain technology into existing enterprise applications. Libraries and SDKs (Software Development Kits) are available to simplify the process of connecting Java applications to various blockchain networks.

3. **Permissioned Blockchains**: In enterprise scenarios, where permissioned blockchains are preferred, Java's security features and enterprise-grade capabilities are valuable. Platforms like Hyperledger Fabric support Java chaincode for developing blockchain applications.

Advantages of Using Java in Blockchain

Java offers several advantages when it comes to blockchain development:

- **Security**: Java's security features, including runtime security checks, memory management, and a strong type system, contribute to more secure blockchain applications.

- **Portability**: Java's "write once, run anywhere" philosophy ensures that blockchain applications developed in Java can run on various platforms without modification.

- **Large Developer Community**: Java has a vast and active developer community. This means more resources, libraries, and support for blockchain developers using Java.

- **Mature Ecosystem**: Java's mature ecosystem includes a wide range of tools, frameworks, and libraries that can be leveraged for blockchain development, reducing development time and effort.

Challenges and Considerations

While Java is well-suited for blockchain development, there are challenges and considerations:

- **Performance**: Blockchain applications often require high throughput and low latency. Java's runtime environment may introduce overhead, so careful optimization is necessary.

- **Ethereum Compatibility**: While Java compatibility with Ethereum is emerging, it's not yet as well-established as Solidity. Developers may need to weigh the benefits of using Java against the existing ecosystem.

- **Resource Consumption**: Blockchain nodes must operate efficiently. Java applications can consume significant resources, so optimizing resource usage is crucial.

In conclusion, Java is increasingly relevant in the world of blockchain, offering security, portability, and a mature ecosystem. Developers looking to enter the blockchain space or integrate blockchain technology into their Java applications will find that Java provides a robust and versatile platform for blockchain development. As the blockchain landscape continues to evolve, Java's role in this domain is likely to expand further.

Section 20.4: The Evolution of Java Language

The Java programming language has undergone significant evolution since its inception in the mid-1990s. In this section, we'll explore the key milestones and changes in the Java language's evolution.

Java 1.0 (1996)

Java 1.0 marked the initial release of Java. It introduced several fundamental features, including the concept of platform independence through the Java Virtual Machine (JVM). Java 1.0 included basic libraries and features like multi-threading, exception handling, and the "applet" concept for web development.

Java 5 (2004) - Generics and Metadata Annotations

Java 5, also known as J2SE 5.0, brought significant enhancements to the language. Two major features stand out:

- **Generics**: Generics introduced the ability to create classes, interfaces, and methods that operate on types as parameters. This improved code safety and reusability.

- **Metadata Annotations**: Annotations provided a way to add metadata to code elements, making it easier to express information about the code, such as its purpose or how it should be processed.

Java 8 (2014) - Lambda Expressions and Streams

Java 8 was a landmark release, introducing several major features:

- **Lambda Expressions**: Lambda expressions allowed developers to write more concise and readable code for handling functions as first-class citizens. This feature enabled the use of functional programming paradigms in Java.

- **Streams**: The Stream API simplified working with collections, enabling developers to process data in a functional, declarative style. It also introduced the concept of parallel streams for concurrent processing.

Java 9 (2017) - Module System

Java 9 introduced the module system, which aimed to improve code modularity and maintainability. The module system allowed developers to define and enforce boundaries between different parts of an application.

Java 11 (2018) - LTS (Long-Term Support) Release

Java 11 was an LTS release, focusing on stability and long-term support. It removed several older features and provided long-term support for the platform.

Java 14, 15, 16 (2020-2021) - Preview Features

Java adopted a faster release cadence, introducing new features every six months. Recent releases included pattern matching, records, and sealed classes as preview features. These features aimed to enhance code readability and maintainability.

Project Loom and Valhalla

Java's future is shaped by ongoing projects like Project Loom, which aims to simplify concurrency with lightweight, user-mode threads (fibers), and Project Valhalla, which explores value types and enhanced data structures.

Conclusion

The evolution of the Java language has been marked by continuous improvement, introducing features that enhance developer productivity, code safety, and performance. Java remains a popular and versatile language used in a wide range of applications, from web development to mobile apps, enterprise systems, and now emerging fields like blockchain and machine learning. Developers can expect Java to continue evolving to meet the demands of modern software development.

Section 20.5: Java's Role in Emerging Technologies

Java, with its rich history and vast ecosystem, continues to play a significant role in emerging technologies. In this section, we'll explore how Java is positioned in various cutting-edge fields.

1. Quantum Computing

Quantum computing is at the forefront of technology, promising to revolutionize computation. While quantum programming languages like Q# and Cirq exist, Java's portability and versatility make it a valuable choice for building software that interacts with quantum computers. Java's adaptability allows developers to integrate quantum libraries and harness quantum computing's potential for solving complex problems efficiently.

2. Augmented and Virtual Reality (AR/VR)

AR and VR technologies are transforming industries such as gaming, education, and healthcare. Java's robust 3D graphics libraries, like Java 3D and jMonkeyEngine, enable developers to create immersive AR/VR experiences. Its cross-platform compatibility makes Java an ideal choice for building AR/VR applications that can run on various devices, including smartphones, headsets, and computers.

3. Blockchain and Cryptocurrency

Blockchain technology is the foundation of cryptocurrencies like Bitcoin and Ethereum, as well as numerous other applications. Java's security features and libraries are well-suited for developing blockchain-based solutions. Developers can build decentralized applications (DApps), smart contracts, and blockchain nodes in Java, ensuring trust and reliability in blockchain networks.

4. Internet of Things (IoT)

The IoT landscape is expanding rapidly, with billions of connected devices collecting and transmitting data. Java's lightweight version, Java ME (Micro Edition), is tailored for IoT applications. It provides a platform-independent environment for developing IoT firmware and embedded systems. Java's support for sensors, low-power devices, and network protocols makes it an excellent choice for IoT development.

5. Artificial Intelligence (AI)

AI and machine learning are driving innovation across industries. While Python is often preferred for AI development, Java is gaining ground. Java libraries like Deeplearning4j and DL4J provide tools for building and deploying AI models. Java's strong typing, performance, and integration capabilities make it suitable for AI solutions, especially in enterprise contexts.

Conclusion

Java's adaptability, reliability, and extensive libraries have enabled it to maintain its relevance in emerging technologies. Its ability to evolve and integrate with new advancements ensures that Java remains a valuable language for developers and organizations looking to stay at the forefront of technological innovation. Whether it's quantum computing, AR/VR, blockchain, IoT, or AI, Java continues to find applications in these exciting fields, contributing to their growth and development.